Managing

Death-Sentenced Inmates:

A Survey of Practices, 2nd Edition

Major Daniel Hudson

FOUNDED 1870

American Correctional Association
Lanham, Maryland

Printed in the United States of America by Graphic Communications, Inc.

ISBN 1-56991-119-3

This publication may be ordered from:
American Correctional Association
4380 Forbes Boulevard
Lanham, Maryland 20706-4322
1-800-222-5646

For information on publications and videos available from ACA, contact our worldwide web home page at: http://www.corrections.com/aca.

Library of Congress Cataloging-in-Publication Data

Hudson, Daniel.
    Managing death-sentenced inmates : a survey of practices / Daniel Hudson.—
2nd. ed
        p. cm.
    Includes bibliographical references.
    ISBN 1-56991-19-3
    1. Prison administration—United States. 2. Death row—United States. 3. Death row inmates—United States. 4. Capital punishment—United States. 5. Executions and executioners—United States. I. Title.

    HV9469 .H8 1999
    365'.6—dc21   99-048232

DEDICATION AND ACKNOWLEDGMENTS

This publication is dedicated to the correctional professionals who work and serve faithfully on the death row and condemned units of the United States of America with commitment and compassion. It also is dedicated to the men and women who serve on the staff of the American Correctional Association representing the correctional professionals throughout the world. And finally, it is dedicated to a very special gentleman who has been my teacher and mentor, "Chappie."

I wish to acknowledge the wardens and superintendents who have allowed me to observe and work with their death row inmates and their staff. I am especially honored to be able to serve as a statewide volunteer in corrections with the states of Illinois and Missouri. I also wish to acknowledge the tremendous encouragement and support I have received in this process of research and the writing of this book by the publications department of the American Correctional Association and that of its publications managing editor, Alice Fins and her staff.

And finally, I wish to acknowledge the help and support of my wife who accompanies me to various correctional centers and prisons. I also wish to recognize my staff who help me to accomplish the tremendous amount of service that we are able to offer to those who are incarcerated.

CONTENTS

FOREWORD

Those who manage inmates sentenced to death have to deal with unique management issues and personal concerns. These arise from the increased number of inmates on a death row, the increased length of time they are there, the pressures of special interest groups, the media, and the public.

Those who are enforced with carrying out this capital punishment verdict must do so with care and professionalism. The American Correctional Association has the following policy on capital punishment—its members are divided on this topic as are most Americans.

PUBLIC CORRECTIONAL POLICY ON CAPITAL PUNISHMENT

Introduction:

Correctional agencies administer sanctions and punishment imposed by courts for unlawful behavior. In some jurisdictions, the law permits capital punishment, and correctional officers have the final responsibility to carry out these executions. Opinions about capital punishment are strongly held, based upon fundamental values about public policy, safety and human life.

There is no uniformity of position about such a controversial issue as capital punishment, either within the corrections profession or as a matter of public opinion at large. A single position for or against capital punishment would not be a fair or candid representation of the range of strongly held and thoughtfully considered positions that exist within the profession.

Policy Statement:

Corrections professionals have a fundamental responsibility to support participation in the public dialogue concerning capital punishment, and to make available to the public and their policy makers the unique perspectives of persons working in the profession. Toward this end, correctional agencies should:

- Support conducting research on capital punishment, to inform the public debate with accurate information about all aspects of capital punishment.
- Support full public discussion of capital punishment, focusing on the morality, purposes, and efficacy of this form of punishment.
- Accept and encourage a diversity of opinion within the field, ensuring employment, promotion and retention are never affected by the expression of an opinion either in support of or opposition to capital punishment.
- Encourage corrections professionals to fully consider the issue, and permit them to present their opinions within the profession and in appropriate public forums.

James A. Gondles, Jr.
Executive Director
American Correctional Association

PREFACE

By reading this work, we hope that you will come to a better understanding of the use of capital punishment in the United States of America. The death penalty was abolished throughout all of Canada in 1976. The information presented has been collected from various state departments of corrections, the Federal Bureau of Prisons, the National Institute of Corrections, the Department of Justice, the military, several cities and counties that have their own death penalty, and various interest groups who are concerned with the use of or the abolishment of the death penalty.

This work is intended to be neither a book of protest nor a book which advocates for the death penalty. Its purpose is to relay the information that has been gained, and to allow correctional practitioners to manage their death row inmates in a legally defensible and humane manner. Readers can make their own judgments on the usefulness of the death penalty in our country.

CHAPTER 1

INTRODUCTION

In 1989, the American Correctional Association published Managing Death-sentenced Inmates—A Survey of Practices. *This publication updates and expands the information that it contained.*

HISTORY OF CAPITAL PUNISHMENT

Throughout the history of the United States, the use of capital punishment has caused tremendous controversy, and it continues to be an issue with which society is intrigued. The death penalty is the most severe punishment that can be imposed. Because it is a final judgment, it continues to generate very heated debate among jurists, legislators, and the general public—including members of the American Correctional Association.

Since the birth of our nation in 1776, several thousand people have been convicted of capital crimes and have been executed by one means or another. As the nation has matured, the imposition of the death penalty has begun to change. For instance, from the time of the Revolution through the late 1800s, nearly all executions were carried out in a public display. However, in the twentieth century, public hangings gave way to state-sanctioned executions, which are conducted in a private chamber within a prison setting.

However, a few public executions continued on an intermittent basis into the 1930s. From the 1930s to the present, executions have been conducted in state or federal prisons in a ritualized process with minimal involvement of the general public.

LENGTH OF TIME ON DEATH ROW

A second important change in the application of the death penalty is the period of time during which an inmate is incarcerated before the actual execution. During the early part of America's history, the appellate process was very limited. Consequently, the time that was spent in a death-sentenced status was relatively short. "Death rows" were limited to one or two people who were held briefly in a local jail before the execution. As time passed, more and varied avenues of legal challenges to the death sentence caused condemned inmates to await execution for longer periods of time. When the American Correctional Association's first book on death-row inmate management was published in 1989, the average time that an inmate spent on a death row or in a condemned unit was seven years (Bureau of Justice Statistics, 1989).

Due to the ever-increasing length of time spent on death row, a death-row unit or condemned gallery is being filled with more inmates than ever before. In 1999, the length of time that an inmate may serve on death row has gone from seven years to an average of thirteen or fourteen years (Illinois Department of Corrections, 1997, 1998). This makes the actual cost of executing an inmate more expensive than it has been in previous years. Many correctional facilities and jurisdictions have reported that these delays are caused by a legal defense strategy that is designed to postpone executions indefinitely.

The existence of death rows in which inmates remain for an extremely long period of time due to the uncertainty of their appeals is a growing phenomenon in American corrections. Before 1976, the average time spent on a death row before execution was approximately thirteen months. The five persons who were executed in 1983 spent an average of four and a half to ten years on death row. The inmates who were executed between 1977 and 1984 spent an average of six years on death row before their executions were carried out (Bureau of Justice Statistics, 1985).

RECORD NUMBER OF EXECUTIONS

The highest recorded number of executions in U.S. history since 1930, when official annual counts began, occurred in 1935 when 199 executions were carried out in the United States (Death Penalty Information Center, 1999). Since 1976, 576 people have been executed in the United States. And, the number of inmates under a sentence of death has continued to grow to 3,517 in 1998 (Death Penalty Information Center, 1977, 1998). In 1960, approximately 200 inmates had a death sentence in our nation's prisons (Bureau of Justice Statistics, 1989). These inmates usually were integrated into the prison's general populations until approximately twenty-four to seventy-two hours before their scheduled executions. Consequently, the management of a separate death row or condemned unit often amounted to supervision in a final holding cell, the last meal, and the execution itself.

Since that time and due to the increasing number of individuals being given the death sentence, various states have had to build a separate death row or condemned unit to house the increasing number of death-row inmates. Illinois, for instance, houses their condemned inmates in three separate prisons and correctional centers (Illinois Department of Corrections, 1998). Table 1.1 shows the number of executions by state over the last twenty-three years.

TABLE 1.1: NUMBER OF EXECUTIONS BY STATE SINCE 1976

Texas	189	[25]	California	7	[2]
Virginia	70	[11]	Indiana	6	
Florida	44	[1]	Utah	5	
Missouri	41	[9]	Mississippi	4	
Louisiana	25	[1]	Nebraska	3	
Georgia	23		Washington	3	
South Carolina	22	[2]	Maryland	3	
Arkansas	21	[4]	Pennsylvania	3	[1]
Alabama	19	[2]	Oregon	2	
Arizona	18	[6]	Montana	2	
Oklahoma	17	[4]	Kentucky	2	[1]
Illinois	12	[1]	Wyoming	1	
North Carolina	13	[2]	Idaho	1	
Delaware	10	[2]	Colorado	1	
Nevada	8	[1]	Ohio	1	[1]

[ ] Denotes 1999 executions
(Source: Death Penalty Information Center, 1999)

STATISTICS ON DEATH-SENTENCED INMATES

By July 1, 1989, the number of inmates who were under the sentence of death had grown from 2,210 people in 34 states to 3,517 in 38 states. (Bureau of Justice Statistics, 1996). This number of condemned inmates is the highest number of individuals on death row since the national count of death-row inmates began. Table 1.2 shows the number of death-sentenced inmates by state. Since 1967, there has been more than a 100 percent increase in the number of death-row inmates, and an overall prison population increase of 61.4 percent (Bureau of Justice Statistics, 1989).

These death-sentenced inmates are being held by the U.S. military, the Federal Bureau of Prisons, and thirty-eight state correctional systems. Two states have capital punishment statutes but have not imposed the death sentence on someone since July 1, 1989 (Bureau of Justice Statistics, 1998).

TABLE 1.2: NUMBERS ON DEATH ROW AND NUMBERS EXECUTED SINCE 1973

State	Under Death Sentence As of 6-1-99			Longest Stay on Death Row (Yrs)	Number Executed Since 1973	Years On Death Row	
	Total	Men	Women			Long (estimate)	Short (estimate)
Alabama	181	179	2	21	18	22	0
Alaska	na	na	na	na	na	na	na
Arizona	115	114	1	20	18	27	7
Arkansas	40	39	1	19	19	18	2
California	539	529	10	21	7	16.8	9.6
Colorado	4	4	0	12.5	1	10	na
Connecticut	5	5	0	9.7	0	na	na
Delaware	18	18	0	17	9	17	3
D.C.	no response						
Florida	376	372	4	26	44	16	2
Georgia	no response						
Hawaii	na	na	na	na	na	na	na
Idaho	20	19	1		1		
Illinois	162	159	3	19	12	17	6
Indiana	46	45	1	20	6	15	1.1
Iowa	na	na	na	na	na	na	na
Kansas	2	2	0	1.3	0	na	na
Kentucky	39	39	0				
Louisiana	81	80	1	16	25	14.3	1
Maine	na	na	na	na	na	na	na
Maryland	17	17	0	18	3	11	4
Massachusetts	no response						
Michigan	na	na	na	na	na	na	na
Minnesota	na	na	na	na	na	na	na
Mississippi	60	59	1	28	4	9	8
Missouri	81	80	1	17	40	15	6
Montana	6	6	0	16	2	20	10
Nebraska	10	10	0	20.9	3	19.4	11.7
Nevada	84	83	1	19.8	8		
New Hampshire	0	0	0	na	0	na	na
New Jersey	15	15	0		0	na	na

State	Under Death Sentence As of 6-1-99			Longest Stay on Death Row (Yrs)	Number Executed Since 1973	Years On Death Row	
	Total	Men	Women			Long (estimate)	Short (estimate)
New Mexico	4	4	0		0	na	na
New York	2	2	0	1	0	na	na
North Carolina	192	188	4	19.6	12	16	2
North Dakota	na	na	na	na	na	na	na
Ohio	196	196	0	17	1	8.9	8.9
Oklahoma	149	146	3	19	17	16.2	2.3
Oregon	25	25	0	8	2	4.5	3.8
Pennsylvania	227	223	4	18	3	13	9
Rhode Island	na	na	na	na	na	na	na
South Carolina	67	67	0	17	22	21	8
South Dakota	3	3	0		0	na	na
Tennessee	101	99	2		0	na	na
Texas	458	450	8	24	177	24.6	69
Utah	12	12	0	16	5	18	4
Vermont	na	na	na	na	na	na	na
Virginia	34	34	0	12.6	67	15.3	1.1
Washington	14	14	0	10.5	3	12.6	2.5
West Virginia	na	na	na	na	na	na	na
Wisconsin	na	na	na	na	na	na	na
Wyoming	2	2	0	1	1	13	13
Federal Bureau of Prisons	20	20	0	11	0	na	na

Source: *Corrections Compendium*, September 1999.

The states of Florida, Texas, and California continue to have the highest numbers of inmates sentenced to death, all with more than 300 inmates each. In 1999, the state of Texas had the highest number—458 inmates under the sentence of death (American Correctional Association, 1999).

As Table 1.2 shows, the states of Kansas, New York, and Wyoming had only two inmates sentenced to death. Despite the death-row inmate population explosion, the actual pace of executions has been slow. In fact, since 1973, as Table 1.2 shows, only twenty-eight of the thirty-eight states with the death penalty actually have used it, and only about half of those have executed more than five condemned inmates.

In 1976, the year of the restoration of the death penalty, there were no executions. Between January 17, 1977, when Gary Gilmore was executed in the state of Utah, and August 1, 1989, 114 men and 1 woman were executed. As of June of 1999, 530 inmates had been executed since 1973. Texas leads the way in executions; 177 inmates have been executed in Texas since 1973. Behind Texas in the number of annual executions are the states of Virginia, Florida, and Missouri, which each has executed forty or more death-row inmates. (American Correctional Association, 1999) (*see* Table 1.2).

Ronald Tabak, who has successfully defended a number of death-sentenced inmates in their appeals, stated that:

> It is possible there will be a significant increase in the number of executions in the next several years . . . [but] even so, it is hard for me to believe that we will actually diminish the number of people on death row. Even if we execute 250 a year—one every weekday of the year—we still wouldn't diminish the death row population. We just won't be adding to it (*Managing Death-sentenced Inmates*, 1989).

Mr. Tabak's statement still holds true today.

How does the United States' rate of executions compare with the execution rate of other countries? In 1998, at least 1,625 prisoners were executed in 37 countries and 3,899 people were sentenced to death in 78 countries, according to Amnesty International (April 1999). This included 68 people who were executed in the United States.

LENGTH OF TIME ON DEATH ROW AND APPEALS

A second trend concerning the population under the sentence of death is the increasing length of time that an inmate spends in a condemned status. The majority of condemned inmates have been under a sentence of death for several years, and the postconviction appellate process will cause many to remain in that status for years to come. Eventually, we will see a domino effect of executions, due to the large number of inmates reaching the end of their appeals.

The current trend is to try and reduce the number of appeals. Presently, there are seven appeals that an inmate may pursue to possibly overturn a death sentence. Some groups and individuals are trying to reduce that number to three appeals to shorten the length of time an inmate is on death row.

Joel Berger of the NAACP Legal Defense Fund states that many death-sentenced inmates not only will be on death row for many years, but never will be executed. Berger cited one study that estimates that in 1980, the overall reversal rate in capital punishment cases was either 60 or 79 percent, depending on the method of calculation (Berger, 1987; *Managing Death-Sentenced Inmates*, 1989). The NAACP Legal Defense Fund records on the reversal rates in capital punishment cases of several state courts of last resort indicate that those rates are often quite high. For example, 38 percent of the 206 appeals decided between 1974 and 1985 by the Texas Court of Criminal Appeals resulted in reversals. Other states in which reversal rates were high include Kentucky (50 percent), Arkansas (37 percent), Tennessee (32 percent), and Nebraska (31 percent) (NAACP Legal Defense Fund, 1987).

In addition to reversals by state appellate court systems, Berger contends that many other death-sentenced inmates eventually will prevail and receive habeas corpus relief in either the Federal District Courts or the Circuit Court of Appeals. He indicates that of 160 capital federal habeas corpus appeals decided across the nation since 1978, 68 have been decided in favor of the condemned inmate, a success rate of 42.5 percent (Berger, 1987). Thus, Berger's data support his contention that many death-sentenced inmates will not be executed and, due to the large labyrinth of legal appeals, most of these inmates will remain on death row for a long time.

As previously noted, in 1976, the median waiting time on death row was thirteen months. For those who have been executed since the death penalty was resumed in 1977, the average time between the imposition of the death sentence and their actual execution was six years and four months. For the eighteen inmates who were executed in 1986, the average length of time they spent on death row was seven years and two months. In 1999, an inmate who was executed in the state of Texas spent almost twenty-five years on a death row unit (Table 1.2, pages 4–5). The trend of lengthening stays on death row units no doubt will continue for the vast majority of the condemned. In 1999, the average waiting time on a death-row unit has been stretched to thirteen to fourteen years.

Comparing inmates who were under the sentence of death in April 1980 and the time of the American Correctional Association/National Institute of Justice survey in 1989, it is noteworthy that only 6 percent of them had been executed, and 40 percent had been removed from death row through means other than execution. In April of 1980, 642 inmates were on death row. Of these, 284 were no longer on death row by 1986. Of the 642 death-sentenced inmates, only 40 inmates had been executed by the end of 1986 (Bureau of Justice Statistics, 1987).

A third concern regarding the management of death-sentenced inmates is the increasing likelihood that their sentences eventually will be carried out. Both condemned inmates and correctional staff have become increasingly aware of the fact that executions are no longer just a possibility, but an actual reality. Because of this, there is a necessity for proper training of the execution team, and proper counseling services for all of those involved in the execution process.

THE AMERICAN BAR ASSOCIATION

Over the years, the American Bar Association has had a great interest in the proper legal representation of individuals who have been sentenced to death. In August of 1986, the staff of the American Bar Association initiated a project on postconviction death penalty representation. The American Bar Association established that 99 percent of those inmates on a death-row unit were indigent and could not afford to pay for proper legal representation for their appeals. This continuing project helps to coordinate emergency placement and supervision of death-row appeals with various bar associations, major law firms, and other interested organizations on a pro bono basis.

Since 1986, the American Bar Association has called for a nationwide moratorium on the use of the death penalty until the death penalty is used in fairness to all. At its February 1997 midyear meeting, the American Bar Association's House of Delegates passed a resolution calling for a halt on executions until the courts across the country can ensure that such cases are "administered fairly and impartially, in accordance with due process," and with the minimum risk of executing innocent people. In 1999, an American Bar Association spokesperson said, "The American Bar Association is still pursuing its quest for a moratorium on the use of the death penalty until Congress can study its usefulness."

The 1997 resolution was adopted by a margin of 280 to 119 votes. The resolution cited some of the American Bar Association's existing policies urging jurisdictions across the country to assure that people who are charged with capital crimes receive due process protections. For example, it would provide competent counsel in capital punishment cases; eliminate race discrimination in capital sentencing; and prevent the execution of mentally retarded persons and persons who committed crimes as minors. However, the resolution also said that the American Bar Association takes no position on the death penalty per se.

CURRENT CONCERNS

Regardless of the reasons for the steady increase in the number of death-sentenced offenders entering the prison system and the relatively small number of executions carried out in a span of years, the situation is becoming more difficult for states with large and growing numbers of condemned inmates. The increasing number of persons on death row and the length of time they spend on death row have created management concerns for correctional administrators and line staff. This also presents new and difficult policy questions for those states with a death penalty and those states that are contemplating the reinstatement of the death penalty.

The need for comprehensive policies and procedures for the management of condemned inmates is evident. The various state departments of corrections are responsible for confining condemned inmates until a decision is reached regarding their final sentence. Should all legal appeals be exhausted (or refused by the inmate) and an execution date set, correctional officials are responsible for carrying out that sentence. Should the inmate have his or her death sentence reduced to that of a term of imprisonment, correctional officials will continue to be responsible for the inmate's incarceration. This means that policies and procedures for condemned inmates need to continue to be developed from the standpoint of long-term correctional assignments. Staffing, security, confinement, and all other factors must be reviewed in terms of inmates who will be under maximum-custody supervision for more than a decade before their final sentence is carried out.

Such concerns raise new and continuous questions about specialized programs for these inmates, such as counseling, education, visitation, recreation, and work assignments. There is a continuous need to define the scope of the death-row inmate management problem, to identify and analyze the programs and services provided to inmates under the sentence of death, and to examine the attitudes of both inmates and the staff who supervise them.

THE AMERICAN CORRECTIONAL ASSOCIATION/ NATIONAL INSTITUTE OF JUSTICE STUDY

Alarmed by the dilemmas created by the growing number of condemned inmates, the American Correctional Association, under the sponsorship of the National Institute of Justice, conducted a study to address the continuing concerns and management of problems regarding those under the sentence of death. This research included the question of whether it is necessary to confine all condemned inmates in one location within an institution. Another question was whether there should be any contact between condemned inmates and the general inmate population. Other issues included the following: What staffing patterns and specialized training are needed for correctional personnel who supervise condemned inmates? What are the legal aspects and liability concerns of death-row inmate supervision? How much out-of-cell time should be allowed to condemned inmates?

These questions, among others, were examined in the study to help correctional administrators examine their current policies or adopt new ones to lead to the efficient operation of the condemned housing units within their institutions. We will attempt to address these questions and see if the various departments of corrections throughout the United States have some policies and procedures worthy of emulation.

DEMOGRAPHIC DATA ON DEATH-SENTENCED INMATES

The American Correctional Association/National Institute of Justice study of 1986 produced data indicating that, in general, a death-sentenced inmate in a correctional facility has the following characteristics:

- Is male
- Has at least a high school education
- Is not married
- Has at least two children who live with their mother
- Has been convicted of murder
- Has appealed the sentence at least twice and has an appeal pending
- Has not been convicted of another crime since first receiving the sentence of death
- Is classified for maximum custody
- Lives in a "death-row housing unit" in a single cell
- Is isolated from general population inmates
- Spends the majority of time sleeping, watching television, working on legal appeals, writing, and reading books
- Is visited mainly by parents, siblings, and friends
- Writes mainly to parents, friends, and lawyers
- Wants to work while in prison, but is not permitted to
- Thinks that death sentences are now more likely to be carried out
- Does not think his or her sentence will be carried out, nor does he or she want it to be

The 3,517 inmates under the sentence of death at the end of 1998 had the following characteristics, according to the Bureau of Justice Statistics (1998):

- Of these inmates, 48 were women and 3,469 were men
- Two out of three had a prior felony conviction
- One out of twelve had a prior homicide conviction
- The racial breakdown of the inmates was as follows: 52 percent were white, 39 percent were black, 7.4 percent were Hispanic, 1 percent were American Indian, and .6 percent were Asian.
- Their average age at the time of arrest was twenty-eight years
- Two percent of the inmates were seventeen years old

- The youngest was seventeen years old
- The oldest was eighty-one years old
- The average education they had was eight and a half years
- One in ten had some college education
- Nearly 50 percent had never been married

The comparison shows that over the years, the educational level of those who are on a death row unit has increased from that of some education to 10 percent with some college education. The racial percentages basically have remained constant. There were several individuals on death row who have had a prior felony conviction and some had a prior murder conviction. Among those now serving time on a death-row unit, more than 50 percent are married and have families.

RACIAL CONCERNS

Is it true that the death penalty verdict is issued more often to African Americans than Caucasians? As Table 1.3 (on page 12) shows, across the nation there are more white inmates on death row than there are black inmates. According to the Bureau of Justice Statistics, in 1996, forty-five persons were put to death by execution. Of those inmates who were executed, thirty-one were white and fourteen were black. In 1966, of the total number of inmates who were on death row, 1,820 were white, 1,349 were black, 24 were Native American, 18 were Asian, and 8 were classified as "other race." Many individuals and organizations compare the number of each category of inmates in a particular race to the population of a particular race within the United States, and on this basis claim that the percentage of a particular race being charged with a capital crime is discriminatory to that particular ethnic group. According to Professor David Baldus in his report to the American Bar Association, quoted by the Death Penalty Information Center, 1999, "In 96 percent of the states where there have been reviews of race and the death penalty, there was a pattern of either race-of-victim or race-of-defendant discrimination, or both."

All individuals made a choice to commit the crime that landed them on death row. The issue is whether others of a different racial background would have been treated differently and received a capital punishment. Whether those crimes are that of white on white, or black on black, or a combination, there are more white inmates on death row in the United States than black inmates. Yet, certain states do have more black inmates on their death rows than white inmates. This poses the question of racial bias in those states regarding handing down of the death penalty at the time of sentencing.

TABLE 1.3: RACE OF INMATES UNDER THE DEATH PENALTY

States	Racial/Ethnic Makeup of Current Death-row Population	Racial/Ethnic Makeup of those Executed Since 1973
Alabama	95 Caucasian; 86 African-American; 1 Asian	6 Caucasian; 12 African-American
Alaska	na	na
Arizona	80 Caucasian; 13 African-American; 18 Hispanic; 4 Native American	13 Caucasian; 3 Hispanic; 2 Native American
Arkansas	17 Caucasian; 22 African-American; 1 Hispanic	14 Caucasian; 4 African-American; 1 Hispanic
California	229 Caucasian; 193 African-American; 97 Hispanic; 23 Asian, Native American and Pacific Islander	5 Caucasian; 1 African-American; 1 Asian
Colorado	1 Caucasian; 2 African-American; 1 Hispanic	1 Caucasian
Connecticut	2 Caucasian; 3 African-American	na
Delaware	9 Caucasian; 9 African-American	5 Caucasian; 3 African-American; 1 Native American
D.C.	no response	no response
Florida	228 Caucasian; 134 African-American; 14 Hispanic	27 Caucasian; 16 African-American; 1 Hispanic
Georgia	no response	no response
Hawaii	na	na
Idaho	20 Caucasian	1 Caucasian
Illinois	51 Caucasian; 103 African-American; 8 Hispanic	7 Caucasian; 5 African-American
Indiana	29 Caucasian; 16 African-American; 1 Hispanic	3 Caucasian; 3 African-American
Iowa	na	na
Kansas	2 Caucasian	na
Kentucky	na	na
Louisiana	23 Caucasian; 57 African-American; 1 Hispanic	13 Caucasian; 11 African-American; 1 Hispanic
Maine	na	na
Maryland	5 Caucasian; 12 African-American	1 Caucasian; 2 African-American
Massachusetts	no response	no response

States	Racial/Ethnic Makeup of Current Death-row Population	Racial/Ethnic Makeup of those Executed Since 1973
Michigan	na	na
Minnesota	na	na
Mississippi	26 Caucasian; 34 African-American	1 Caucasian; 3 African-American
Missouri	45 Caucasian; 36 African-American	22 Caucasian; 18 African-American
Montana	5 Caucasian; 1 Caucasian/Native American	2 Caucasian
Nebraska	8 Caucasian; 1 African-American; 1 Native American	1 Caucasian; 2 African-American
Nevada	45 Caucasian; 34 African-American; 5 Hispanic	Unknown
New Hampshire	na	na
New Jersey	9 Caucasian; 6 African-American	na
New Mexico	3 Caucasian; 1 Hispanic	na
New York	1 African-American; 1 Hispanic	na
North Carolina	78 Caucasian; 105 African-American; 7 Native American; 2 Elias Syrian/Angel Guevara	12 Caucasian
North Dakota	na	na
Ohio	94 Caucasian; 97 African American; 5 Hispanic	1 Caucasian
Oklahoma	84 Caucasian; 48 African-American; 1 Asian; 6 Hispanic; 9 Native American; 1 Iraqi	13 Caucasian; 1 African-American; 1 Asian; 1 Hispanic; 1 Native American
Oregon	22 Caucasian; 2 Hispanic; 1 Native American	2 Caucasian
Pennsylvania	72 Caucasian; 140 African-American; 2 Asian; 13 Hispanic	3 Caucasian
Rhode Island	na	na
South Carolina	33 Caucasian; 34 African-American	14 Caucasian; 8 African-American
South Dakota	3 Caucasian	na
Tennessee	64 Caucasian; 33 African-American; 1 Asian; 2 Hispanic; 1 Native American	na

States	Racial/Ethnic Makeup of Current Death-row Population	Racial/Ethnic Makeup of those Executed Since 1973
Texas	167 Caucasian; 190 African-American; 97 Hispanic; 4 other	90 Caucasian, 56 African-American; 29 Hispanic; 2 other
Utah	7 Caucasian; 2 African-American; 2 Hispanic; 1 Native American	3 Caucasian; 2 African-American
Vermont	na	na
Virginia	17 Caucasian; 17 African-American	31 Caucasian; 34 African-American; 2 Hispanic
Washington	11 Caucasian; 3 African-American	2 Caucasian; 1 Hispanic
West Virginia	na	na
Wisconsin	na	na
Wyoming	2 Caucasian	1 Caucasian
Federal Bureau of Prisons	5 Caucasian; 14 African-American; 1 Asian	na

Source: *Corrections Compendium*, September 1999.

CHAPTER 2:

LEGAL ISSUES

LEGAL PROTECTIONS FOR DEATH-ROW INMATES

By the 1930s, a series of U.S. Supreme Court decisions broadened the legal protections that were to be extended to death-sentenced inmates. The Supreme Court had become increasingly sympathetic toward the rights of capital defendants. A number of major Supreme Court decisions outlined the constitutionally required legal protections for inmates under the sentence of death. In *Powell v. Alabama*[1] (1932), the high court held that capital-punishment defendants must be provided counsel. In subsequent decisions, the high court provided protection against coerced confessions (*Fikes v. Alabama*, 1957) and ruled that jurors who expressed moral or religious objections to capital punishment could not be excluded from capital juries (*Witherspoon v. Illinois*, 1968).

In 1972, the Supreme Court, by a five-four vote, in a landmark decision, *Furman v. Georgia*, ruled that capital punishment as practiced in the United States violated the Eighth and Fourteenth Amendments of the Constitution.

Specifically, the high court ruled that the death penalty had been used in an arbitrary, capricious manner, thereby violating the constitutional guarantees against cruel and unusual punishment. This decision invalidated all death-penalty laws in America. Therefore, many states quickly moved to revise their capital punishment statutes to satisfy the objections that were raised by the Supreme Court. In 1972, more than 600 inmates were under the sentence of death, and all of them had their death sentences reduced to imprisonment for life without parole (Bureau of Justice Statistics, 1989).

In 1976, the Supreme Court reversed itself, in part, with *Gregg v. Georgia*, which held that states, indeed, may execute murderers providing that certain procedural safeguards were met. For instance, the court struck down mandatory death sentence statutes and the imposition of the death sentence

---

[1] *Full legal citations on page 91.*

for rape. Since that time, various laws and statutes have been passed to include the death penalty for certain sexual crimes. In 1977, the moratorium on capital punishment ended with the execution of Gary Gilmore in the State of Utah. Gary Gilmore, in his quest to die, waived his right to appeal, which drew a great deal of attention. From January 1977 to August 1989, there were 115 executions in 13 states. Then, other states slowly began to conduct executions as well. Since that time, 530 inmates have been executed in 34 states (Death Penalty Information Center, 1998, 1999).

Due to the ever-increasing growth in the number of death-sentenced inmates in this country, combined with the extreme nature of the sentence, we need to look at the death penalty in more detail. The litigation of death-penalty cases takes many forms, which affect those individuals whose job it is to manage condemned inmates.

Some states have had litigation which resulted in consent decrees or some other level of legal agreement, such as *Daniels v. Zant* (Georgia), *Thompson v. Enomoto* (California), *Groseclose v. Dutton* (Tennessee), and *Rust v. Gunter* (Nebraska). Other cases that have been filed either have been dismissed or are still pending. Several of these cases offer insight into the evolving legal standards for managing inmates under the sentence of death. Death-row inmates have filed numerous lawsuits to gain some dignity and be treated as human beings even while on the death-row unit. Because of this, states have experienced a tremendous rise in their legal costs to defend such cases. This has forced some states to seek legislation to bar many of these cases as frivolous. Other states have turned to the accreditation process, which is operated by the Standards Department of the Americn Correctional Association, as a means to ensure their facilities, including their death-row facilities, meet at least minimum standards. In many cases, accreditation has meant fewer law suits and a more effectively run prison.

Several death penalty cases again are before the Supreme Court. Decisions are expected in 2000 and may have a significant impact on the method of execution, and the length of time inmates are on death row.

As Table 2.1 illustrates, after the death penalty was ruled unconstitutional in 1973, several states rewrote their death penalty acts to make them comply with the Supreme Court ruling. Delaware was a state that did not have the death penalty prior to the ruling but now has the law on its books. On the other hand, nine states that had the death penalty before 1973 now do not have it. These states include the following: Alaska, Hawaii, Iowa, Maine, Minnesota, Rhode Island, Vermont, West Virginia, and Wisconsin. Alaska and Maine are considering reinstating the death penalty. Additionally, Massachusetts, Michigan, North Dakota, and the District of Columbia do not have the death penalty. Table 2.2 shows the states which have proposed changes in their death penalty.

TABLE 2.1: DEATH PENALTY LEGISLATION

States	In Effect	In Effect- Since 1973	States	In Effect	In Effect- Since 1973
Alabama	Y	Y	Nebraska	Y	Y
Alaska	N	Y	Nevada	Y	Y
Arizona	Y	Y	New Hampshire	Y	Y
Arkansas	Y	Y	New Jersey	Y	Y
California	Y	Y	New Mexico	Y	Y
Colorado	Y	Y	New York	Y	Y
Connecticut	Y	Y	North Carolina	Y	Y
Delaware	Y	N	North Dakota	N	N
D.C.	N	No Response	Ohio	Y	Y
Florida	Y	Y	Oklahoma	Y	Y
Georgia	No Response		Oregon	Y	Y
Hawaii	N	Y	Pennsylvania	Y	Y
Idaho	Y	Y	Rhode Island	N	Y
Illinois	Y	Y	South Carolina	Y	Y
Indiana	Y	Y	South Dakota	Y	Y
Iowa	N	Y	Tennessee	Y	Y
Kansas	Y	Y	Texas	Y	Y
Kentucky	Y	Y	Utah	Y	Y
Louisiana	Y	Y	Vermont	N	Y
Maine	N	Y	Virginia	Y	Y
Maryland	Y	Y	Washington	Y	Y
Massachusetts	N	No Response	West Virginia	N	Y
Michigan	N	N	Wisconsin	N	Y
Minnesota	N	Y	Wyoming	Y	Y
Mississippi	Y	Y	Federal Bureau of Prisons	Y	Y
Missouri	Y	Y			
Montana	Y	Y			

Source: *Corrections Compendium* September 1999.

In 1999, a number of states expanded the crimes that can be considered capital felonies or added new aggravating circumstances. For example, in Connecticut, the charge of capital felony was expanded to include imprisoned persons who murder a corrections department employee or other person providing services for the department. Four states changed their methods of execution to lethal injection. (Turpin and Lyons, 1999).

Table 2.2: Proposed Changes in Death Penalty Methods of Execution

States	Changes	Moratorium Proposals	Death Penalty Options Life Without Parole	Straight Life
Alabama	None being considered	None	Y	N
Alaska	Abolished in 1957; being reconsidered	NA	NA	NA
Arizona	Eliminated in 1972; reinstated 1973; ruled unconstitutional in 1978; reinstated in 1979	None	Y	N
Arkansas	Reinstated in 1973; no changes being considered	None	Y	Y
California	None being considered	None	Y	Y
Colorado	None being considered	None	Y	Y
Connecticut	Reinstated in 1973; no changes being considered	None	Y	Y
Delaware	None being considered	None	Y	NA
D.C.	No Response			
Florida	Reinstated in 1976; add lethal injection; shorten appeal time	None	Y	Y
Georgia	No Response			
Hawaii	None being considered	NA	NA	NA
Idaho	Reinstated in 1977; no changes being considered	None	Y	Y
Illinois	Reinstated in 1977; no changes being considered	Yes, one year proposed	Y	N
Indiana	Reinstated in 1977; no changes being considered	None	Y	Y
Iowa	Eliminated in 1964; no changes being considered	NA	Y	N
Kansas	Reinstated in 1994; no changes being considered	None	N	N
Kentucky	Reinstated in 1976; no changes being considered	Yes, to life without parole	Y	NA
Louisiana	Reinstated in 1976; no changed being considered	Yes, to indefinite term	Y	N

States	Changes	Moratorium Proposals	Death Penalty Options Life Without Parole	Straight Life
Maine	Death penalty provisions not used since late 1800s; changes being considered in the current legislature	NA	NA	NA
Maryland	Reinstated in 1987; no changes being considered	None	Y	Y
Massachusetts	No Response			
Michigan	NA	NA	Y	Y
Minnesota	Eliminated in 1911 and unused since 1906; no changes being considered	NA	Y	Y
Mississippi	Reinstated in 1977; no changes being considered	None	Y	NA
Missouri	Reinstated in 1977; no changes being considered	None	Y	Y
Montana	No changes being considered	Yes, two years proposed	Y	Y
Nebraska	Reinstated in 1976; no changes being considered	Yes, three years proposed	Y	Y
Nevada	Reinstated in 1979; no changes being considered	None	Y	Y
New Hampshire	No changes being considered	None	Y	Y
New Jersey	Reinstated in 1982; changes being considered in current legislature	None	Y	Y
New Mexico	Reinstated in 1979; no changes being considered	None	N	NA
New York	Reinstated in 1995; changes being considered in current legislature	None	Y	Y
North Carolina	Reinstated in 1977; changes being considered in current legislature	None	Y	Y
North Dakota	NA	NA	Y	Y
Ohio	Reinstated in 1981; no changes being considered	None	N	N

| States | Changes | Death Penalty Options | | |
		Moratorium Proposals	Life Without Parole	Straight Life
Oklahoma	Reinstated in 1977; no changes being considered	None	Y	Y
Oregon	Reinstated in 1984; no changes being considered	None	Y	NA
Pennsylvania	No changes being considered	Yes, unspecified	Y	Y
Rhode Island	Eliminated in 1852	None	N	N
South Carolina	Reinstated in 1977; no changes being considered	None	Y	Y
South Dakota	Reinstated in 1979; no changes being considered	No	Y	Y
Tennessee	No changes being considered	No	Y	Y
Texas	No changes being considered	No	N	N
Utah	No changes being considered	No	Y	Y
Vermont	Eliminated in 1966; no changes being considered	NA	Y	N
Virginia	Reinstated in 1978; no changes being considered	No Response	Y	Y
Washington	No changes being considered	No	Y	N
West Virginia	Eliminated in 1969; no changes being considered	NA	NA	NA
Wisconsin	NA	NA	Y	Y
Wyoming	No changes being considered	No	Y	Y
Federal Bureau of Prisons	Reinstated in 1998, changes being considered	No	Y	NA

Source: *Corrections Compendium*, September 1999.

Not all legislation that favors the death penalty or results in more stringent and harsh measures of correctional actions passes (*see* Lauen, 1997 for a discussion of these phenomena). In March 1999, a bill to reintroduce the death penalty in Massachusetts was defeated by seven votes despite the strong support from Governor Paul Cellucci, according to *Death Penalty News* (June 1999).

In May 1999, the Nebraska state legislature became the first in the United States to pass a bill calling for a two-year moratorium on executions in its state. The moratorium would have allowed a study to be made as to whether the death penalty was being applied fairly in the state and, while death sentences still could have been handed down, none would have been carried out. However, Governor Mike Johanns vetoed the bill stating, "the death penalty is the law of Nebraska. We have an obligation to enforce that law."

DNA TESTING

Three-hundred and fifty people convicted of capital crimes in the United States between 1900 and 1985 were innocent of the crimes charged, according to a 1987 study. Some prisoners escaped execution by minutes, but twenty-three were actually executed. A U.S. Congressional report by the House Subcommittee on Civil and Constitutional Rights in October 1993 listed forty-eight condemned men who had been freed from death row since 1972. The report blamed inadequate legal safeguards to prevent wrongful executions and listed numerous inherent flaws in the criminal justice system. The report concluded "Judging by past experience, a substantial number of death row inmates are indeed innocent and there is a high risk that some of them will be executed."

In recent years, issues concerning the use of DNA testing have arisen because innocence or guilt can be validated through such tests. In the past five years, in many instances, an inmate on a death row has been able to get DNA testing and when the results were released, the inmate has been released immediately because the test showed the inmate's innocence.

Under a 1999 Illinois law, the state is required to perform DNA testing on a defendant in the pretrial stage of the case, thereby proving evidence of the accused's innocence or guilt before the case actually goes to trial. This should be of great benefit to the individual death-row inmate, since the cost of such testing is extremely expensive. The emerging question is who will be responsible for such testing for those inmates already on a death row?

The *New York Times* reported in March 1998 that new DNA evidence taken from the exhumed body of Dr. Sam Sheppard provides the most compelling evidence that he was wrongfully convicted of murdering his wife in 1954 in Ohio. The prosecution had sought the death penalty for Dr. Sheppard, but he was given a life sentence after one of the most sensational trials of the century. His conviction was overturned, and he was acquitted at his retrial. This case was the basis for a popular TV series and a recent movie, *The Fugitive*. In another example, recent DNA evidence tends to squelch lingering suspicions that Dr. Sheppard was guilty of murdering his wife and points to a former window washer at the Sheppard residence who is imprisoned for another murder.

MENTAL RETARDATION AND
MENTAL COMPETENCE

The general legal principle is that a state cannot execute those inmates who have lost their ability to comprehend their impending death or the reasons for it. Therefore, the methods to test and assess the sanity of an inmate with a death-sentence are receiving greater review and scrutiny from the legal system all the way up to the Supreme Court. Recent cases illustrate that this sanity test should be of a judicial nature and not an administrative decision.

In April of 1999, Nebraska enacted a law that prevents the execution of persons who are mentally retarded. Under the law, an IQ of 70 or less on a reliably administered test would be presumptive evidence of mental retardation. Nebraska is the twelfth state in the United States to adopt such a law. The other states that prohibit the execution of the mentally retarded include the following: Arkansas, Colorado, Georgia, Indiana, Kansas, Kentucky, Maryland, New Mexico, Tennessee, and Washington. New York also prohibits execution of the mentally retarded except for murder by a prisoner. The United Nations' Special Rapporteur in his fifteenth annual report to the United Nations condemned the United States practice of imposing the death penalty on those who are mentally retarded. However, to date, thirty-four offenders in the United States who were mentally retarded have been executed (Death Penalty Information Center, 1999).

An analysis of the consistent standards that are seen in precedent-setting cases may help in writing guidelines that will pass constitutional muster. Throughout the country, the various departments of corrections along with state legislators have an obligation to continue to develop written policies that address the purpose and needs of death-row inmate management. The need for such policies exists regardless of the size of the jurisdiction or of the death-sentenced population. We will look at issues that already have been litigated and then examine those issues that currently are under consideration.

ORIENTATION

It is important that written procedures be in place to ensure inmates' proper orientation regarding their death-row status. These procedures relate to the need for separating such individuals from the general inmate population, and from other death-sentenced inmates during the initial reception and orientation phase. At this stage, many inmates are given a written document explaining their rights and the expectations of the facility. It is important that these procedures and guidelines are explained properly by trained staff so the administration is not vulnerable to legal action, which could be brought if preventive measures and guidelines are not in place.

Typically, written procedures for death-row inmates include methods and timetables for documentation of the inmates' criminal history. They also include a special needs assessment. These procedures are based on the proper training of staff members who are responsible for completing each orientation component.

CLASSIFICATION

The process for classification is a factor in a number of legal cases such as *Daniels v. Zant*. However, there seems to be a lack of classification assessment tools necessary to make a proper assessment of a death-sentenced inmate. In some cases, classification is used to determine which inmates can have meals outside their cells or attend group religious services. In some jurisdictions that allow some death-sentenced inmates to work, classification is used to assign "work capable" status to certain condemned inmates.

In general, legal consent agreements state that classification is most critical in those jurisdictions where some inmate activities are group-based or involve integration with other death-sentenced inmates. Classification status is linked to recreation, program participation, out-of-cell meals, program service availability, and off-tier work participation. Where integration into the general inmate population occurs for some or all inmates under the sentence of death, classification plays a critical role in the everyday operation of a death-row unit.

Classification is especially necessary where prisons, such as in Missouri, are forced to use double-bunking in their cells. This has resulted in the development of classification-assessment tools and processes to lead to better cell assignments. With the death-row populations in some states surpassing 300 or more inmates, it is unlikely that a group of this size can be managed effectively without some organized attempt to classify death-sentenced inmates for custody, programs, and service needs.

None of the court cases that have been noted has provided legal standards or guidelines on the nature and/or extent of the classification process for these units. Therefore, each department of corrections should develop, or continue to develop, an assessment tool to provide a proper classification for those who are under a death sentence. Due to the long time in which a death-row inmate is in a condemned unit, an assessment and classification procedure needs is necessary

PERSONAL HYGIENE AND PROPERTY

Many lawsuits have addressed issues of personal hygiene and property. Other cases have concerned the conditions of confinement. The reason for what may appear as excessive attention to these areas may be the combination of the need for elevated security for this group and the extra legal and public scrutiny that is given to them. While these court cases have not suggested specific guidelines in these areas, they have demonstrated the need for specific written policies that address detailed property rights (or definitions of contraband), procedures to deal with property and property rights during the transfer of death-sentenced inmates, the provision for receiving property gifts during family visits, restrictions of property related to hygiene such as razors and so on, codes for hair length and style, and religious or medical exceptions to these rules.

Although many state departments of corrections have developed a list of property items which inmates may have in their possession, the general public, including an inmate's immediate family, is not made aware of what the inmates may have in their possession or in their cell. Because of this, many institutions and staff have encountered problems with family members trying to bring items that are considered contraband into the institution. The excuse then becomes "it is the inmate's responsibility to inform those who visit with them on what they may be allowed to accept and receive." The problem with this is that the property guidelines of many institutions constantly are changing, according to the security needs of that particular institution. Until consistency and stabilization comes to the inmate property list, this will continue to be a concern that will need to be examined.

RECORDS

Most often, the maintenance of various records is addressed in legal cases on the conditions of confinement. The records provide liability protection for the department of corrections and the staff. In the review of the policies and procedures of the various departments of corrections, there is a definite paper trail of records necessary for the protection of each agency as a whole. The various critical components of these records include the following:

- A unit logbook
- Incident reports
- Use-of-force reports and documentation
- Minutes of classification meetings
- Notes on procedures
- Disciplinary write-ups or tickets
- Documentation of administrative segregation or other status changes
- Requests and responses to requests for protective custody
- Medical intervention
- Records of other specialized programs or services
- Staff training records

With the use of computers and better record keeping, it is extremely important that all records be reviewed by the proper staff members concerning the daily operation of the prison. It is better never to assume that someone has made the proper entry into the daily records. Many times, situations arise on a death-row unit that call staff members away from their everyday desk duties and later, an individual's memory may be fallible, and the person may not make a proper entry. Extreme care should be taken to see that the proper entries are made on a timely basis.

FOOD SERVICE

In addition to litigation addressing the general conditions of confinement, there are cases involving the food service policies of various institutions concerned with the death-row unit. Many cases have been filed for inmates who seek to have their meals served in a dining area rather than in their cell.

Food service and its delivery are critical to administrators of units for death-sentenced inmates because of its connection with institutional security. Within these special units, which in many jurisdictions are quite small, separate food service to this group poses many challenges for the administration.

Meals for death-sentenced inmates most often are prepared and delivered from a central kitchen of the prison, and then served by either security staff or specially picked inmates to those inmates serving time on a death row. The food service sections in many policy manuals spell out in great detail the procedures regarding the timing of meals, response expectations when disturbances take place, specialized meal needs for religious or medical purposes, and special security issues that are connected with the food services, such as paper plates for assaultive inmates, utensil counts, the hoarding of food, and so forth.

Many of the food issues surface in older facilities where there is more of a security risk to the line officers and maintenance workers. In more modern structures, security measures are in place to handle the various types of classifications of death-row inmates and to see to their needs for proper meals and food services.

MEDICAL SERVICE

Most cases on conditions of confinement involving inmates under the sentence of death have sections dealing with the medical treatment of such inmates. Most cases of litigation allege the lack of medical treatment for those who are confined on a death row.

As a general procedure, it is preferable to be able to provide medical care to each inmate in his or her cell because of the specialized security needs that usually result when a death-sentenced inmate must be removed from the cell or housing unit to go to the institution's medical unit or to an outside medical center. When these instances arise, most procedures assign a line officer to the medical department to handle the proper searches and related security matters. It is extremely important that this officer be trained in working with medical staff to be able to make the security risk as minimal as possible. Telemedicine may be a viable option for many death-sentenced inmates.

LEGAL SERVICES AND ACCESS TO THE LAW LIBRARY

The best available guideline for law library access comes from Nebraska's *Rust v. Gunter* case. This plan calls for death-sentenced inmates to be allowed the opportunity to visit the law library at least two hours per day, five days per week. Frequently, units for death-sentenced inmates either have established their own law library or have designated an inmate adviser who may be responsible for these requests or materials on a one-to-one basis. Table 2.3 provides information on how each state handles issues of legal assistance. Most use a law library and outside legal counsel.

The general legal principle is that a death-sentenced inmate has the right to have access to the institution's court-appointed attorney on an individual basis, on request. Related issues are addressed in conditions of confinement suits, as well as the *Brisbon v. Lane* case (attorney visits). In the more infrequent situations where transportation to the law library is permitted, detailed procedures must specify the security measures, such as the use of restraints and timetables for the use of the law library. Major jurisdictional variations in library procedures and access are connected with both the facility's size and whether the library is located on or off of the death-row housing unit.

For cases that involve a library on the unit, separation of individual inmates is accomplished through use of a schedule and a timetable. In cases involving a library that is not located on the unit, escort and search procedures are needed.

With the use of computers, many institutions have modernized their law libraries and cut down on the space that is needed for the housing of books and bookshelves. However, no correctional department allows inmates to have access to the Internet. However, to offer limited computerized service to the death row, only a small space is needed within a housing unit.

TABLE 2.3: LEGAL ASSISTANCE TO DEATH-ROW INMATES

States	Legal Assistance	States	Legal Assistance
Alabama	Library; outside attorneys	Kentucky	Law library; outside attorneys; inmate legal counsel
Alaska	NA		
Arizona	Outside attorneys; contract paralegal	Louisiana	Law library; outside attorneys; inmate legal counsel
Arkansas	Law library; outside attorneys	Maine	NA
California	Law library; outside attorneys; "pocket" law libraries in two facilities	Maryland	General library; outside attorneys; inmate legal counsel; Maryland law on CD-Rom; dayroom computer; librarian visits daily; LASI, PSIM
Colorado	Law library (without physical access); outside attorneys; inmate legal counsel		
		Massachusetts	No Response
Connecticut	Outside attorneys; inmate legal counsel; loose collection of legal books	Michigan	NA
		Minnesota	NA
		Mississippi	Outside attorneys
Delaware	Law library; outside attorneys	Missouri	Law library; outside attorneys; inmate legal counsel
D.C.	No Response		
Florida	Law library; outside attorneys	Montana	Law library; outside attorneys
Georgia	No Response	Nebraska	Law library; outside attorneys; inmate legal counsel; university law school
Hawaii	NA		
Idaho	Outside attorneys; paralegals		
Illinois	Law library; outside attorneys; inmate legal counsel; inmate law clerk	Nevada	Law library; outside attorneys
		New Hampshire	Law library; outside attorneys; inmate legal counsel
Indiana	Law library; outside attorneys; inmate legal counsel	New Jersey	Outside attorneys; inmate legal counsel
Iowa	NA	New Mexico	Law library; outside attorneys; inmate legal counsel
Kansas	Law library; outside attorneys; inmate legal counsel; Legal Services for Prisoners, Inc.	New York	Law library; outside attorneys

States	Legal Assistance	States	Legal Assistance
North Carolina	Outside attorneys; inmate legal counsel	Texas	Law library; outside attorneys; inmate legal counsel
North Dakota	NA		
Ohio	Law library; outside attorneys	Utah	Outside attorneys
		Vermont	NA
Oklahoma	Law library; outside attorneys	Virginia	Law library; outside attorneys
Oregon	Law library; outside attorneys; inmate legal counsel	Washington	Law library; outside attorneys; inmate legal counsel
Pennsylvania	Law library, with inter-library loan services; inmate legal counsel	West Virginia	NA
		Wisconsin	NA
Rhode Island	NA	Wyoming	Law library; outside attorneys
South Carolina	Law library; outside attorneys	Federal Bureau of Prisons	Law library; outside attorneys; inmate legal counsel
South Dakota	Outside attorneys; inmate legal counsel		
Tennessee	Law library; outside attorneys; inmate legal counsel		

Source: *Corrections Compendium*, September 1999.

RECREATION

The most frequently addressed issue in death-row litigation is recreation. This high level of legal activity might suggest guidelines are developing, but this is not necessarily true. There are continuing differences in the definitions of what recreation is and the connection that it has to the classification process.

The amount of time that death-row inmates are allowed outside of their cells for recreational activities is a continuing issue raised in various litigation. Some jurisdictions call all out-of-cell time "recreation." Other jurisdictions divide this time into an exercise period, mealtime (where meals are received out of the cell), work time (where this is permitted), and similar divisions of out-of-cell activities. Table 2.4 provides some definitions of what various states consider "recreation."

TABLE 2.4: RECREATION PROGRAMS FOR DEATH-ROW INMATES

States	Recreation	States	Recreation
Alabama	Outside yard, inside day room, TV, radio	Maine	NA
Alaska	NA	Maryland	Outside yard; inside dayroom, including TV and VCR, board games and cards; TV; radio
Arizona	Inside concrete pen		
Arkansas	Outside yard, 12 hours per week in 2 hr increments	Massachusetts	No Response
		Michigan	NA
California	Outside yard, inside dayroom, TV, radios, chess, cards, board games, basketball, no free weights	Minnesota	NA
		Mississippi	TV; radios
		Missouri	Outside yard; inside dayroom; TV; radio
Colorado	Exercise yard; TV	Montana	Outside yard; inside dayroom; TV; radio (all depending on behavior)
Connecticut	Exercise yard; inside dayroom; TV; radios		
Delaware	Outside yard; inside dayroom; radios	Nebraska	Outside yard; inside dayroom; TV; radio; books, magazines, newspapers
D.C.	No Response		
Florida	Outside yard; TV		
Georgia	No Response	Nevada	Outside yard; inside dayroom; TV; radio
Hawaii	NA		
Idaho	Outside yard; inside dayroom; TV and radio (if purchased from commissary)	New Hampshire	Outside yard; inside dayroom; TV; radio
		New Jersey	Outside yard; inside dayroom; TV; radio; word processor
Illinois	Outside yard; inside dayroom; TV; radio	New Mexico	Outside yard; TV; radio
Indiana	Outside yard; inside dayroom; TV; radio	New York	Outside yard; TV on the unit
Iowa	NA	North Carolina	Outside yard; inside dayroom, with TV; radio
Kansas	Outside yard; TV; radio; hobby craft; books; phone		
		North Dakota	NA
Kentucky	Outside yard; TV; radio	Ohio	Outside yard; inside dayroom; TV; radio
Louisiana	Outside yard; radio; tier time; TV outside cells		

States	Recreation	States	Recreation
Oklahoma	Outside yard/ inside dayroom (females); Exercise yard for men inside a building with mesh screen on top for openness; TV; radio	Texas	Outside yard; inside dayroom
		Utah	Outside yard; inside dayroom; TV (for some); radio
Oregon	Outside yard; TV; radio; open area on tier with tables	Vermont	NA
		Virginia	Unavailable
Pennsylvania	Outside yard; inside dayroom; TV; radio	Washington	Outside yard; inside dayroom; TV and radio (earned privileges)
Rhode Island	NA		
South Carolina	Outside yard; TV (if incarcerated pre-1995)	West Virginia	NA
		Wisconsin	NA
South Dakota	Outside yard; TV; radio	Wyoming	Outside yard; TV; radio
Tennessee	Outside yard; inside dayroom; TV; radio	Federal Bureau of Prisons	Outside yard; TV; radio; inside recreation

Source: *Corrections Compendium*, September 1999.

Some states have their own classification for their inmates who are under the sentence of death, and those that do tend to differentiate among inmates who are entitled to recreation and for how long rather than relying on a global, across the board standard for all inmates in this status. A look at variations in existing consent decrees will help pinpoint these differences.

The *McDonald v. Armontrout* case in Missouri develops provisions for indoor and outdoor recreation. Missouri mainstreams their death-sentenced inmates into the general population housing units. The decision provides for phased-in increases in recreation time of at least thirty-two hours per week. It also addresses the possibility of phased-in increases in the size of recreational groups of at least four inmates, and renovations in both indoor and outdoor recreational facilities for death-sentenced inmates.

While the *McDonald v. Armontrout* case stipulates a mixture of inmates during recreational time, it is in contrast with the trend toward maximum separation of individual inmates in this status. However, it is noteworthy that Virginia inmates who are given a death sentence are allowed out of their cells in groups of six or seven from 8:00 A.M. to 8:00 P.M. daily (NAACP Legal Defense Fund, 1986). They also are allowed to eat meals outside of their cells, are allowed to attend group religious services, and are allowed to receive ten hours of outdoor recreation per week.

The consent agreement of *Daniels v. Zant* in Georgia in 1981 guaranteed a minimum of thirty-two hours per week of out-of-cell time, and it guaranteed a minimum of at least six hours per week of outdoor exercise. While the decree did not specify the size of the recreational area, it does specify the equipment that can be used including softballs and gloves, footballs, basketballs, and volleyball equipment. This out-of-cell time is linked to the classification used in the prison and for attendance at religious services and similar activities by those who are under the sentence of death. In many correctional centers and penal institutions, the time that is used by an inmate in religious activities is charged against the number of hours of out-of-cell time.

In other states, death-sentenced inmates are given a varying number of hours per day for recreation. These time periods range from six hours per day of out-of-cell time, seven days a week, to twelve hours of outdoor recreation time per week. The process and procedures of various jurisdictions spell out the exact rules for the timing and the location for recreation.

Often, special procedures are required for those death-sentenced inmates who have a special status (for example, protective custody, orientation, disciplinary detention, or a medical restriction). Where inmates do not exercise separately from others, rules for the grouping of inmates are extremely important in the state's written policy for the handling of death-sentenced inmates. This is equally true for the specificity required for body searches before and after recreation, the process for refusal, and even the procedures for the changing of channels when television viewing is classified as recreation. Some states only allow one death-row inmate at a time to go into a specified exercise yard. After being bodily searched, the inmate has the right to refuse to go into the yard and has the right to return to his or her cell and give up recreation time.

Most jurisdictions allow death-row inmates to exercise in the outside yard, but most do not specify either for how long they can exercise nor whether they exercise in small groups or as individuals. As Table 2.4 shows, most jurisdictions also specify recreation in the dayroom. No jurisdiction mentions allowing death-sentenced inmates to use an inside gym. A large number of jurisdictions allow inmates to watch television or listen to radios, but whether this is in their cell or in a dayroom is unclear. In California, death-sentenced inmates are allowed to play chess, cards, board games, and basketball.

For recreation, the issue is how much time is allowed outside and how much time is allowed inside. Then, the issues concern whether inmates are allowed individual televisions and/or radios and other hobby items. In

Florida, "each death row inmate has an individual black and white television in their cell while regular population inmates have color televisions in a common day room. Death row inmates do not have the opportunity for idle time out of their cell as is enjoyed by open population inmates" (Association of State Correctional Administrators, 1992). Table 2.5 (page 33) shows the amount of time each state allows death-sentenced inmates to be outside of their cells.

VISITATION

Most jurisdictions have very detailed procedures on who is permitted to visit a death-sentenced inmate, the number of visitors allowed at one time, the conditions of the visitation—contact or noncontact, and the timetable for these events both in the days that inmates may have visitors and the number of hours for such visits. Missouri allows up to seven hours and Alabama, Florida, Kentucky, and Nevada allow up to six hours, as Table 2.6 shows.

Institutions throughout the country vary on whether they permit visits to take place in the same area as that used for the general population visits (in which case the policies establish separate times), or in a section or area that is used only for death-sentenced inmates. Each jurisdiction also has procedures for moving to and from these areas and procedures for searching inmates and their visitors.

One problem of most jurisdictions regarding visitation concerns whose responsibility it is to inform family members and friends about the proper procedures and rules for such visits. Although many institutions post these rules on a bulletin board in the visiting room for visitors to see and in the gatehouses of each institution, many visitors do not have access to a copy of these rules before they attempt to visit with their loved one. This poses the need for properly trained personnel who know how to work with the general public in a congenial way, particularly with those who are making a visit for the first time. In those institutions where more modern search equipment is available at the front gate, and where the staff is able to greet the general public in a very professional way, many visitation confrontations have been avoided.

COUNSELING SERVICES

The legal aspects of counseling services appear to be contingent on the definition given of "counseling" in institutional policies. In some cases, "counseling" focuses on a role that is traditionally attributed to a caseworker, while in other institutions, the role is reserved for the psychologist and related mental health staff serving the institution.

(continued on page 38)

TABLE 2.5: MOVEMENT ALLOWED OUTSIDE OF CELL PER DAY

States	Allowed Outside Cell Per Day	States	Allowed Outside Cell Per Day
Alabama	Under 1 hr	Nebraska	2 hrs
Alaska	NA	Nevada	3 or more hrs
Arizona	1 hr, 3 per week	New Hampshire	3 or more hrs
Arkansas	3+ hrs	New Jersey	2 hrs; inside and outside recreation every other day
California	Maximum of 6 hrs, 7 days per week, depending on inmate	New Mexico	Varies based on classification
Colorado	1 hr		
Connecticut	1 hr outside rec; 1 hr in evening; phone calls, work duties, visits	New York	1 hr
		North Carolina	3 or more hrs
		North Dakota	NA
		Ohio	1 hr
Delaware	1 hr	Oklahoma	1 hr, five days per week for exercise; 3 times (15 min) per week for showering
D.C.	No Response		
Florida	Twice weekly for 2 hrs each		
Georgia	No Response	Oregon	2 hrs
Hawaii	NA	Pennsylvania	1 hr five days per week
Idaho	1 hr	Rhode Island	NA
Illinois	Varies from 1-3 hrs by facility	South Carolina	1 hr
		South Dakota	45 minutes recreation per weekday
Indiana	3 or more hours		
Iowa	NA	Tennessee	Varies depending on program level
Kansas	1 hr		
Kentucky	1 hr normally, but can vary	Texas	Varies based on classification*
Louisiana	1 hr	Utah	Varies based on classification
Maine	NA		
Maryland	3 or more hrs	Vermont	NA
Massachusetts	No Response	Virginia	Unavailable
Michigan	NA	Washington	1 hr
Minnesota	NA	West Virginia	NA
Mississippi	1 hr	Wisconsin	NA
Missouri	3 or more hrs	Wyoming	1 hr 15 min
Montana	1 hr	Federal Bureau of Prisons	2 or more

*provided November 1999.

Source: *Corrections Compendium*, September 1999.

TABLE 2.6: VISITING POLICY FOR DEATH-ROW INMATES

States	Visitations-Number per Week	Visitations-Length in Hours	Visitations-Type
Alabama	1	6	Contact
Alaska	NA	NA	NA
Arizona	Up to 5	2, unless special	Noncontact
Arkansas	1	3	Contact, depending on inmate
California	4	Varies by space available and number of visitors at a given time	Grade "A" inmates, contact, grade "B" inmates, noncontact
Colorado	1	4	Noncontact
Connecticut	3	1	Contact for legal; noncontact for social
Delaware	1	1	Noncontact
D.C.	No Response	No Response	No Response
Florida	Socially on weekends	6	Contact or non-contact, depending on inmate
Georgia	No Response	No Response	No Response
Hawaii	NA	NA	NA
Idaho	No Response	NA	Noncontact
Illinois	2	2, if space available, or 1 if segregation status	Contact or non-contact, depending on inmate
Indiana	No limit	2-4, if space available	Contact
Iowa	NA	NA	NA
Kansas	1.5	3.5 mornings and 2.5 afternoons	Noncontact
Kentucky	1	6	Contact
Louisiana	2 per visitor/month; 10 visitors on list per inmate	2-4	Contact or non-contact, depending on inmate
Maine	NA	NA	NA
Maryland	8 per month	30 minutes	Noncontact
Massachusetts	No Response	No Response	No Response
Michigan	NA	NA	NA
Minnesota	NA	NA	NA
Mississippi	1	1	Noncontact
Missouri	20	7	Contact
Montana	5	NA	Noncontact

States	Visitations- Number per Week	Visitations- Length in Hours	Visitations- Type
Nebraska	2	2.8	Contact, but could vary, depending on inmate
Nevada	2	6	Contact
New Hampshire	2	1	Noncontact
New Jersey	2	1	Noncontact
New Mexico	Unlimited	2	Depends on the inmate
New York	1	Several hours	Contact
North Carolina	NA	NA	Noncontact
North Dakota	NA	NA	NA
Ohio	3; 5 maximum per month	3	Noncontact
Oklahoma	8 per month and state holidays	2	Noncontact
Oregon	2 on weekends	2 2hr family visits	Noncontact
Pennsylvania	1	1 hr, unless extended to 2 hrs with approval	Noncontact
Rhode Island	NA	NA	NA
South Carolina	First come first served	2	Noncontact
South Dakota	2	Varies	Noncontact
Tennessee	2, males; of the two current females on death row, one can have two visits per month of two visitors for two hours and the second female follows the guidelines of the general population	1-3 hrs, males	Depends on the inmate
Texas*	Varies based on classification	2	Noncontact*
Utah	1	1.5	Noncontact
Vermont	NA	NA	NA
Virginia	Unavailable	Unavailable	Unavailable
Washington	2	2 approximately	Noncontact
West Virginia	NA	NA	NA
Wisconsin	NA	NA	NA
Wyoming	1	2	Noncontact
Federal Bureau of Prisons	2 plus legal	2 for social	Noncontact for social, may be contact for legal

*information updated November 1999.
Source: *Corrections Compendium*, September 1999.

TABLE 2.7: RELIGIOUS AND MENTAL HEALTH COUNSELING FOR DEATH-ROW INMATES

States	Counseling— Religious	Counseling— Mental Health
Alabama	General population chaplain	Y
Alaska	NA	NA
Arizona	General population chaplain; contractors/ community volunteers	Y
Arkansas	General population chaplain	NA
California	General population chaplain	Y
Colorado	General population chaplain; outside ministers; volunteers	Y
Connecticut	General population chaplain	Y
Delaware	General population chaplain; outside ministers with warden's consent	Y
D.C.	No Response	No Response
Florida	Death row chaplain; general population chaplain; outside ministers	Y
Georgia	No Response	No Response
Hawaii	NA	NA
Idaho	Outside ministers	Y
Illinois	Death row chaplain; general population chaplain; outside ministers; volunteers	Y
Indiana	Death row chaplain; outside ministers	Y, upon request or recommendation
Iowa	NA	NA
Kansas	General population chaplain; outside ministers if on visiting list	Y, if requested or need observed by staff
Kentucky	General population chaplain; outside ministers	Y
Louisiana	Death row chaplain; outside ministers	Y
Maine	NA	NA
Maryland	General population chaplain; outside ministers	Y
Massachusetts	No Response	No Response
Michigan	NA	NA
Minnesota	NA	NA
Mississippi	General population chaplain	Y
Missouri	Death row chaplain; general population chaplain; outside ministers	Y

States	Counseling—Religious	Counseling—Mental Health
Montana	General population chaplain	Y
Nebraska	General population chaplain assigned to entire institution	Y
Nevada	General population chaplain; outside ministers	Y
New Hampshire	General population chaplain; outside ministers	Y
New Jersey	Death row chaplain	Y
New Mexico	General population chaplain; outside ministers	Y
New York	General population chaplain	Y
North Carolina	Death row chaplain	Y
North Dakota	NA	NA
Ohio	General population chaplain; outside ministers	Y
Oklahoma	General population chaplain; outside ministers; volunteers	Y
Oregon	General population chaplain; outside ministers	Y
Pennsylvania	General population chaplain	Y
Rhode Island	NA	NA
South Carolina	Death row chaplain; general population chaplain; outside ministers	Y
South Dakota	General population chaplain; outside ministers, if on visiting list	Y
Tennessee	Death row chaplain; outside ministers	Y
Texas	Inmate may choose an advisor who does not count towards general visits	Y
Utah	General population chaplain	Y
Vermont	NA	NA
Virginia	General population chaplain	Y
Washington	Death row chaplain; outside ministers, depending on religious preference	Y
West Virginia	NA	NA
Wisconsin	NA	NA
Wyoming	General population chaplain	Y
Federal Bureau of Prisons	General population chaplain; Closed-circuit TV available for BOP-recognized faith groups	Y, thorough mental health exams every 30 days or sooner

Source: *Corrections Compendium*, September 1999.

Regardless of these distinctions, a review of the written polices and discussion with staff clearly demonstrates that in death-sentenced inmate management, most staff members and inmates feel a great need for these kinds of services. The counseling needs of such inmates seem to be concerned with the anticipation of execution, the uncertainty of their appeal in the legal system, and their separation from the general population. Table 2.7 shows what each system allows. Other legal considerations arise from the need for specialized counseling services for staff and other inmates when an execution is carried out.

In many jurisdictions, the chaplain of the institution is left out of the counseling process, and counseling is limited to the mental health staff. However, the death-row inmate, who has a certain date and time for his or her death, will face the dilemma of the death and grief process as anyone else who may be dying of a terminal disease. In many cases, a religious counselor or a chaplain is called on to help such individuals with their acceptance and knowledge of dying.

In a recent death-penalty case in Illinois, a volunteer chaplain was subpoenaed to testify as to the spiritual commitment that a death-row inmate had made in his life. This testimony was used to make the determination as to the inmate's acceptance of his death and execution.

RELIGIOUS SERVICES AND ACTIVITIES

Many states have a death row chaplain to handle religious counseling. Others employ the regular prison chaplain in this role. Still others use outside religious leaders or a combination of all three.

Along with education and recreation, religious services and activities are programs most requested by inmates on death rows. Most inmates have reported that the current practice of religious services and activities include Bible study groups, religious worship services, and visits with chaplains. A large number of death-row inmates have indicated that they would like to have programs such as church services with different clergy, religious education, and additional Bible studies. Many inmates report that they would like to attend religious worship services in a chapel or in a specially designated place for religious services on the death-row unit. Death-sentenced inmates report that Bible study is one of the top four activities on which they spend the majority of their time.

The passage of the Religious Freedom and Restoration Act (RFRA) has created a number of concerns about religious activities in a prison setting. Since prisoners on death row rank religious study and services to be of such importance, this causes great concern for issues of death-row inmate management. The requests and demands of inmates' new religious groups may cause serious security concerns. In some instances, a new religious group has been questioned as to its validity as an organized and recognized religion.

The chaplain can play an important role during and after the execution. The office of the chaplain can provide support to staff, inmates, and the condemned. The condemned inmate may want baptism or communion hours before death.

The chaplain has a vital role in dealing with the inmate. This includes grief preparation, including writing a will, and writing letters to family and victims. It is important, according to a National Institute of Corrections seminar, to provide the inmate with a detailed description of what will happen. The chaplain also should help the inmate to plan his or her own funeral. They may meet with a funeral director, choose burial clothes, discuss disposition of any money, and depending on the policies and regulations discuss autopsy and donation of organs (*see* page 39 on organ donation).

The inmate may request the delivery of letters to the victim's family and/or other inmates they know at the prison, and the disposition of personal property such as a Bible and jewelry. Sometimes the inmate may choose to make a last statement, though this is prohibited in some states. The inmate also may request special religious last rites. At times, there may be unusual requests such as making a video to be shown later to children or for special visits. The inmate may request the dignity of wearing special clothing at the time of execution.

The chaplain plays a role for inmates in the general population and in the death row for those who are curious about what is happening to another inmate. It is important, according to the National Institute of Corrections, to validate their right to feel in a structured and reasonable manner. Inmates close to the condemned person may experience a reaction and need to discuss this issue with the chaplain. It is important not to just ignore the death row inmates and other inmates; do not try to cut them off totally from the television and newspapers or their ability to talk to the staff.

CHAPTER 3

SPECIAL ISSUES
AND CONCERNS

Through the review of literature, the site visits, the discussions with correctional staff, analysis of the data collected through the American Correctional Association, and through information provided by death-sentence tracking organizations, we identified a number of special issues and concerns.

HEALTH ISSUES

According to a National Institute of Corrections' seminar, medical personnel face the ethical dilemma of actually keeping the condemned person "healthy" enough to kill and being some part of the execution later. Similarly, the mental health staff is faced with the issue of preventing depression and suicide so that the execution may occur. The mental health staff may be asked to do a psychological examination for the purposes of commutation. The medical staff may need to decide on the use of medication during the death watch. It may be wise to consider using contractual medical personnel for the medical opinion needed to verify that death has occurred. *See* Faiver (1998) on this issue.

When a medical person is called on to administer the lethal injection, the American Medical Association has developed a position for its physicians on their role in the execution process and the procedures that must be taken into consideration as a member of the medical profession. According to a spokesperson for the American Medical Association, it is up to individual doctors to make their own choice as to their employment with a department of corrections

The American Correctional Health Services Association, an affiliate of the American Correctional Association, voted to take the following position on September 22, 1991, according to *Corhealth*, August-Oct. 1991:

The ACHSA Board of Directors supports the right of noncondemned prisoners to voluntarily donate organs during life or at the time of death. We are opposed to organ donation by condemned prisoners, since such a policy would result in medicalizing executions, would be seen as mitigating the impact of execution, and would also be in violation of our provisional code of ethics which prohibits health professionals from being involved in any aspect of implementation of the death penalty.

RELATIONSHIP WITH THE INMATES' FAMILY

According to the National Institute of Corrections, "at times, the inmates' family will turn to and identify with the prison staff as they have visited over the years and have developed relationships with the prison staff. Expect requests from the family to see and talk with the warden in the last weeks." Talking with the warden is very important and appropriate. They need the attention of the warden in charge and not only the chaplain, although it is vital that they do have access to the chaplain, as well.

The correctional administration needs to plan the last visit and decide whether it will be a contact visit. A National Institute of Corrections' seminar suggested that it should be a contact visit for the sake of the family but there are a number of security considerations that need to be made.

"Plan for the night of the execution," the seminar suggests. Many family members will want to be at the prison. The correctional administration must decide where they will be and who will be with them. "Try to allow them to leave the prison after the execution quietly and privately." It is important to prepare the family ahead of time for searches, and other procedures they will undergo at the prison, especially if they have not been there previously. Another issue is whether family members will be witnesses, a procedure that several states do not allow.

HOUSING AND CELLS

In the housing area, beyond whether the inmates are segregated in a death row, there is the question of whether they are single celled or double celled. Florida in its death row fact sheet states that a death row cell is six by nine by nine-and-a-half feet high. The death watch cell (where the inmate is brought when the governor signs a death warrant on him or her) is twelve by seven by eight-and-a-half feet high (1991).

In Texas, prisoners will spend up to twenty-three hours a day in a room about six-and-a-half feet wide and ten feet long, with a built-in toilet and small sink, a bunk and two shelves. Each cell has a slit-like window that lets in a bit of sunlight, but no air. The door is solid steel with a pair of vertical slits that serve as windows. Another slit—hinged and horizontal—serves as the gate for food trays (Stewart, 1999). In the new death row in the Terrell Unit, in a high-security administrative segregation building, death row inmates will have air that is cooled to 85 degrees. The death chamber is at a separate unit and prisoners will be moved there shortly before their execution.

Table 3.1 provides information on the specific death row unit or units in each state (information on housing of women is included in the section in this chapter on women on death row). All systems use individual cells, except for Oklahoma and Missouri that have double bunking. In Pennsylvania, death row inmates are in five separate special housing units.

An analysis of the written policies of departments of corrections clearly illustrates that a consensus exists among correctional administrators that inmates with a death sentence should be housed in an area that has minimal contact with the general prison population. Although the nature and extent of possible death-sentenced populations seem to be growing, the integration of such inmates with other inmates still remains a very controversial issue. Policies vary widely regarding contact with other inmates and staff both on and off the death-row unit, yet legal guidelines in these areas are minimal or nonexistent.

Of all of the states that have a death-row unit, only one, Missouri, mainstreams condemned inmates with others within the prison confines. Tennessee allows their female death-row inmates to commingle based on their behavior. However, at the present time, Tennessee only has two women on death row. The Missouri Department of Corrections places their condemned prisoners in various housing units throughout its maximum-security prison. The corrections department has found that these individuals show a sense of calmness and well-being in their incarceration. These inmates are allowed to have certain work assignments throughout the prison, which gives them an opportunity to give something back to the community. In interviewing several of the staff members of this prison, many commented that in the beginning they did not believe that this practice would work, but they have learned that it does work for all who manage such inmates.

PROCEDURES

In reviewing the written policies of the various states and the guidelines of their department of corrections, it is apparent that their policies have been reviewed very carefully and updated on a continual basis to satisfy any litigation that might be considered on behalf of the death-row inmate.

TABLE 3.1: DEATH PENALTY FACILITIES

States	Specific Death Row Unit(s)	States	Specific Death Row Unit(s)
Alabama	Yes, 3 facilities	New Jersey	Yes, self-contained unit (single lock)
Alaska	NA		
Arizona	Yes, separated from general population	New Mexico	Yes, north unit of state penitentiary
Arkansas	Yes, specific unit	New York	Yes, section of maximum security facility
California	Yes, in one facility		
Colorado	No specific unit	North Carolina	Yes, separate sections and floors of pods
Connecticut	Yes, in cells separated by divider wall	North Dakota	NA
Delaware	No specific unit	Ohio	Yes, maximum security cell block at a different prison than where sentence is carried out
D.C.	No Response		
Florida	Yes		
Georgia	No Response	Oklahoma	Yes, separate high security area, including administrative segregation
Hawaii	NA		
Idaho	Yes, a tier at maximum security unit	Oregon	Yes, tier in disciplinary segregation unit at state penitentiary; overflow in administrative segregation
Illinois	Yes, 3 facilities		
Indiana	Yes, 4 separate cell blocks		
Iowa	NA	Pennsylvania	Yes, special housing units at 5 institutions
Kansas	No	Rhode Island	NA
Kentucky	Yes, in general population cell house, segregated by safety glass and confined	South Carolina	Yes, separated from general population
		South Dakota	Yes, separated from general population
Louisiana	Yes, 1 cell block		
Maine	NA	Tennessee	Yes, one unit containing four pods
Maryland	Yes	Texas	Yes, a series of attached cells
Massachusetts	No Response		
Michigan	NA	Utah	NA
Minnesota	NA	Vermont	Yes
Mississippi	Yes, in a maximum security unit	Virginia	Yes
		Washington	Intensive Management Unit first year and special unit determined by behavior
Missouri	No separate unit		
Montana	No separate unit		
Nebraska	Yes, same as for general population but reserved for death row	West Virginia	NA
		Wisconsin	NA
		Wyoming	Yes, isolated in separate block
Nevada	Yes		
New Hampshire	Yes, section of maximum security facility	Federal Bureau of Prisons	Yes, one special confinement unit

Source: *Corrections Compendium*, September 1999.

CUSTODY AND SECURITY

In most jurisdictions, written procedures for custody and security appear to be based on the traditional needs of a high-security death-row unit operating twenty-four hours a day on a continuous basis. Most of these units seem to be operating in older facilities, which have a minimal amount of high-tech security.

However, in those facilities where a death-row unit is housed in a more high-tech facility, the written procedures for such institutions are designed to meet the specialized needs of this population. This includes provision for more legal visits with attorneys, possible media interaction, and specific consequences of escape. Such procedures require the implementation of very specialized training for the staff who work on units where death-sentenced inmates are housed. Such training should include skills to be able to work with those who would come in from the outside (lawyers, counselors, chaplains, and so on) and those who are part of the everyday operational staff.

The written procedures for security and custody also specify timetables and positions for the posting of officers, shift duties, lines of command and communication, and procedures for the transfer and movement of both death-sentenced inmates in general, and those presenting special management needs and problems, such as disruptive inmates or individuals who are contemplating suicide.

Where these guidelines and procedures have been developed and maintained, there seems to be a lack of litigation. However, in units where litigation has addressed the shortcomings of certain systems, more clear and precise guidelines seem to follow.

SPECIALIZED PROGRAMS

To the correctional practitioner dealing with the management of death-sentenced inmates, the increased length of time they are on death row dictates the need for specialized programs for condemned inmates that strike a balance between prison operations and security and the inmates' need to avoid deteriorating mentally and physically while awaiting the final disposition of their sentences.

The history of permitted activities in Texas illustrates what was common across the country for death-sentenced inmates. Prior to 1993, death row inmates were largely confined to their cells in Texas, as elsewhere. The only out-of-cell activity permitted was recreation, which was limited to one hour per day, seven days a week. Inmates were permitted to bathe daily, one at a time on their cellblocks. Job assignments, educational opportunities and other activities we perceive today as normal daily functions were denied all inmates under a sentence of death. *See* Table 2.3 in Chapter 2 for a description of recreation programs.

These strict guidelines reflected a philosophy that death row inmates had to be segregated for security purposes. All inmates so sentenced were deemed to be high escape risks and were thought more likely to inflict physical injury on another inmate or an officer (National Institute of Corrections, 1993). Canada, by contrast, has a best practices program, Lifelines, in which lifers work outside the prison (Rhine, 1998).

As a result of a lawsuit concerning the conditions of confinement on death row, the State of Texas initiated a three-month experimental program for death-row prisoners. The state agreed that inmates in the general population with a longer criminal history and more horrendous crimes than some of those assigned to a death row were holding jobs, so the state agreed to classify death-row prisoners into two categories: work-capable and others. Those work-capable inmates were given significant additional freedom of movement and access to activities and assigned regular prison jobs, equivalent to duties assigned to general population inmates. However, with a change in director, who believed that death-row inmates should be restricted in their jobs because they were inciting individuals in the general population to disruptive behavior, the amount of work allowed death-row inmates became very limited.

In 1986, Texas opened the first prison industry shop ever to employ only death-row inmates as its workforce. An indirect product of the reforms ordered by the U.S. District Court in *Ruiz v. Estelle*, the Ellis I Death Row Garment Factory successfully merged the inmates' need for meaningful out-of-cell activity with the production of goods which directly benefits the state (NIC, 1993). At present, however, all jobs are suspended.

WORK PROGRAMS

As Table 3.2 illustrates, a few states allow their death-row inmates to be part of work programs. In many of the programs, the inmates must work in their pods or are restricted in their contacts to the special housing unit. For example, in Colorado, Connecticut, and Maryland, death-row inmates may work as barbers or janitors in their pods. In Nebraska and New Mexico, such inmates may work as porters. In the Federal Bureau of Prisons, death-sentenced inmates may work as laundry orderlies and sewing machine operators.

TABLE 3.2: WORK PROGRAMS FOR DEATH PENALTY INMATES

States	Work Programs	States	Work Programs
Alabama	No	New Mexico	Unit porters
Alaska	NA	New York	No
Arizona	No	North Carolina	No
Arkansas	2 hour shifts, if approved	North Dakota	NA
California	No	Ohio	May apply for unit jobs on a 6-month rotating basis
Colorado	May apply as barbers or janitors in their pods		
		Oklahoma	No
Connecticut	Cleaning details; barbers	Oregon	Custodial on tier
Delaware	No	Pennsylvania	Yes, but restricted to special housing unit
D.C.	No Response		
Florida	No	Rhode Island	NA
Georgia	No Response	South Carolina	No
Hawaii	NA	South Dakota	No
Idaho	No	Tennessee	Level A inmates have first choice, primarily custodial; 20 are assigned to prison industries doing data entry
Illinois	No		
Indiana	For limited number		
Iowa	NA		
Kansas	No	Texas	Garment factory; SSI orderlies or clerks; barbers (but all jobs currently suspended)
Kentucky	Yes, but jobs cannot interact with general population		
Louisiana	No	Utah	Pending
Maine	NA	Vermont	NA
Maryland	Barbers and sanitation	Virginia	Unavailable
Massachusetts	No Response	Washington	Special housing units and possibility of stamping return address on envelopes
Michigan	NA		
Minnesota	NA		
Mississippi	No	West Virginia	NA
Missouri	Yes	Wisconsin	NA
Montana	In the school	Wyoming	No
Nebraska	Porter duties on a rotating basis	Federal Bureau of Prisons	Phases I and II programs offering opportunities such as laundry orderlies and sewing machine operators
Nevada	No		
New Hampshire	Sewing project		
New Jersey	No		

Source: *Corrections Compendium*, September 1999.

TABLE 3.3: EDUCATION PROGRAMS FOR INMATES ON DEATH ROW

States	Education	States	Education
Alabama	Unavailable	Nevada	Correspondence
Alaska	NA	New Hampshire	Regular classes
Arizona	Correspondence; institutional TV	New Jersey	Individual tutoring
Arkansas	Available upon request and approval	New Mexico	Regular classes via ETV; correspondence; individual tutoring
California	Correspondence; outside college courses offered by satellite	New York	In-cell study
		North Carolina	Correspondence, at inmate's expense
Colorado	Regular classes; individual tutoring; GED preparation; ESL; post high school classes	North Dakota	NA
		Ohio	Correspondence; individual tutoring
Connecticut	Correspondence; or via assigned teacher	Oklahoma	Correspondence; material provided for self-study; GED preparation
Delaware	None		
D.C.	No Response	Oregon	Materials for self-study, if requested
Florida	None		
Georgia	No Response	Pennsylvania	Basic literacy; post-secondary opportunities at inmate's expense; ABE; GED preparation; self-study program
Hawaii	NA		
Idaho	TV programming		
Illinois	Correspondence		
Indiana	Correspondence	Rhode Island	NA
Iowa	NA	South Carolina	Unavailable
Kansas	Individual tutoring; GED preparation	South Dakota	None
		Tennessee	Maximum security level would require individual tutoring
Kentucky	Correspondence		
Louisiana	Correspondence; literacy course with staff supervision	Texas	None
		Utah	Correspondence
Maine	NA	Vermont	NA
Maryland	Correspondence	Virginia	Unavailable
Massachusetts	No Response	Washington	Correspondence
Michigan	NA	West Virginia	NA
Minnesota	NA	Wisconsin	NA
Mississippi	Correspondence	Wyoming	Regular classes; correspondence
Missouri	Regular classes; correspondence; individual tutoring	Federal Bureau of Prisons	Closed-circuit TV for educational programming
Montana	Self-study		
Nebraska	Correspondence; individual tutoring		

Source: *Corrections Compendium*, September 1999.

EDUCATION

As Table 3.3 shows, correspondence courses are the most prevalent type of education available to death-row inmates. However, some states provide regular classes for the inmates and others allow individual tutoring. The need for programs is especially acute for those inmates who have been placed on death-row units but later have been released to the general public due to new evidence that has proven their innocence.

In North Carolina, James French, deputy warden, explained that "death-row inmates are offered the DARE-TV program (Development and Remedial Education Television). This program allows inmates to have access to educational programming through closed-circuit television" (Association of State Correctional Administrators, 1992).

REMOVAL FROM DEATH-SENTENCED STATUS

Although the number of inmates who are being placed on death rows is growing, history reveals that a large proportion of those inmates with death sentences eventually will be removed from that status and not by the carrying out of the death penalty. Joel Berger of the NAACP Legal Defense Fund maintains that many inmates on a death-row unit will win their cases and will have their death sentence reduced to life in prison or lesser terms of imprisonment. Deaths among this population due to executions, suicides, natural causes, and assaults (between 1973 and 1989) represent only 9 percent of the dispositions that took inmates off of the death-sentenced inmate rolls (NAACP Legal Defense Fund, 1989).

SUPERMAX FACILITIES

With the truth-in-sentencing laws now in place, the use of the various life-imprisonment terms will cause various jurisdictions to look at the need for more and larger maximum-security prisons. Many state legislators have allocated funds to build bigger and more secure facilities to be operational in the next few years. At the present time, there is a rise in the construction of "closed supermax" facilities. In 1999, more than thirty states operated one or more units or facilities specifically for their corrections systems' most threatening inmates, according to Morris Thigpen, Director of the National Institute of Corrections (Riveland, 1999). In these facilities, the movement of inmates is very minimal and security is very tight.

Such facilities are designed to restrict the general movement of inmate populations as a group. Yet, the American Civil Liberties Union and others see the isolation of inmates in such facilities as cruel and unusual punishment. Because of this, many individuals and groups have petitioned against the building of such facilities. There is a great concern about the mental, physical, and spiritual condition of both regular inmates and the death-row inmates who are serving time in such closed supermax facilities.

The *Rights for All* publication of Amnesty International states:

> The authorities in charge of supermax units should amend their policies to ensure that no prisoner is confined long-term or indefinitely in conditions of isolation and reduced sensory stimulation.

In the early penitentiaries, the leading criminologists and religious reformers thought that if individuals could spend time alone repenting for their crime, they would come out of prison better persons. Instead, many of the prisoners went crazy due to the isolation of their confinement. Similar results are occurring in some of the maximum-security prisons that house death row inmates.

According to Amnesty International, the authorities should improve conditions in such units so that prisoners have more out-of-cell time; better access to fresh air and natural light; improved exercise facilities; increased association with other inmates, and access to work, training, or vocational programs; and are not held in windowless cells. The mentally ill or those at risk of mental illness should be removed from supermax units. The authorities should establish clear criteria for and regular review of placement in supermax units (Amnesty International, 1998, p. 85).

Correctional practitioners and inmates serving their time on a death-row unit expect that there will be disturbances which will involve people being assaulted or injured. With this in mind, those who are responsible for designing and building such facilities are now building facilities with more up-to-date security systems to handle such inmates.

In older facilities, most inmates are housed on a gallery with open bar cell doors, which have to be unlocked by an individual with a key. However, in the newer modern facilities, inmates are housed in a direct supervision pod with electronic doors, which are opened and closed through a computerized system. A direct supervision pod is more easily controlled for security purposes. Those individuals who have been able to tour such facilities will understand the difference.

As Riveland notes (1999):

> Security issues clearly become the focal point of most extended control facilities. . . . Many security issues are dependent upon the physical design, and proper design can go a long way in ameliorating many security problems. However, the greatest contribution to a sound security program is an alert, well-trained professional staff. With few exceptions, escapes, disturbances, and homicides in extended control facilities were the result of human error.

The routine inherent to these facilities can become disarming, leading to a potential breakdown in critical procedures. Some agencies, by policy or scheduling, attempt to lessen the effects of routine by rotating staff in the housing units, between units, and into other parts of the facility. Frequent shakedowns of the cells and areas of the facility that inmates may use are essential and require extensive staff training and supervision if they are to be conducted properly.

EXECUTION POLICIES AND PROCEDURES

Several factors have evolved in the development of execution policies and procedures. At the present, several states with capital punishment statutes have not actually carried out an execution because the death sentence has not been handed down by the courts of those states. Of the thirty-eight states that currently have death penalty statutes, only twenty-nine have executed someone since 1977.

There are differences in the current inmate populations and execution practices, which have made the execution policies and procedures written decades ago out of date and in some cases, no longer applicable. As Riveland notes (1999):

A formal, official, frequent, and ongoing updating of policies and procedures is essential. Informal exceptions, handwritten modifications, and memoranda at variance with existing policies or procedures quickly render them ineffective, if not useless. If operations or incidents are challenged in court, the facility's policies and procedures will become its greatest ally or greatest adversary.

One of the policy changes concerns the method of execution, which has changed over time. Because of this, several policies have changed to allow the inmates choices among the various methods of execution. As Table 3.4 shows, thirty-four states and the Bureau of Prisons use lethal injection, ten states used electrocution, three states use the gas chamber, two states use hanging, and two states use a firing squad. Most of these states have the choice of lethal injection, as well as the other methods mentioned. However, in those states in which another method other than lethal injection is used, the inmate being executed sometimes will choose another method, such as Gary Gilmore of Utah, who chose to be executed by a firing squad.

Because of the problems the state of Florida has had with its electric chair, on their web page they provide the following information about the electric chair:

TABLE 3.4: METHODS OF EXECUTION

States	Methods of Execution and those Charged with Conducting the Executions	States	Methods of Execution and those Charged with Conducting the Executions
Alabama	Electric chair; by staff	Kentucky	Electric chair and lethal injection (injection added in 1998)
Alaska	NA		
Arizona	Gas; lethal injections added in 1992; by staff	Louisiana	Lethal injection; changed from electric chair; confidential sources
Arkansas	Electric chair; lethal injection added in 1993; by staff and outside person		
		Maine	NA
		Maryland	Lethal injection; changed from gas; by staff
California	Lethal injection; gas if inmate requests; by staff		
		Massachusetts	No Response
Colorado	Lethal injection; gas added in 1988; by staff	Michigan	NA
		Minnesota	NA
Connecticut	Lethal injection since 1995; by staff and/or outside person	Mississippi	Lethal injection; by staff and/or outside person
		Missouri	Lethal injection; by staff
Delaware	Lethal injection since 1986; by hanging unless injection requested and if sentenced previously; by staff	Montana	Lethal injection; changed from hanging; by staff and/or outside person
		Nebraska	Electric chair; by confidential sources
D.C.	No Response		
Florida	Electric chair; by staff and private citizen (executioner)	Nevada	Lethal injection; changed from gas; by staff
		New Hampshire	Lethal injection added in 1986 or by hanging; by staff
Georgia	No Response		
Hawaii	NA		
Idaho	Lethal injection or firing squad; hanging eliminated 1973	New Jersey	Lethal injection; changed from electric chair in use from 1907 to 1972; by discretion of the Commissioner
Illinois	Lethal injection; changed from electric chair in 1983; by staff		
		New Mexico	Lethal injection; by outside persons
Indiana	Lethal injection; changed from electric chair in 1995	New York	Lethal injection; changed from electric chair; by staff
		North Carolina	Lethal injection; changed from gas; by staff
Iowa	NA		
Kansas	Lethal injection; changed from hanging in 1993	North Dakota	NA

States	Methods of Execution and those Charged with Conducting the Executions	States	Methods of Execution and those Charged with Conducting the Executions
Ohio	Electric chair or lethal injection, at inmate's option; by staff	Utah	Lethal injection or firing squad; eliminated hanging; by staff and outside person
Oklahoma	Lethal injection; by outside person	Vermont	NA
Oregon	Lethal injection, used for first time in 1996; by staff and/or outside person	Virginia	Lethal injection; electric chair if original sentence so states or by injection at inmate's option; by staff
Pennsylvania	Lethal injection, changed from electric chair in 1990; by outside person	Washington	Lethal injection; or hanging at inmate's option; by outside person
Rhode Island	NA	West Virginia	NA
South Carolina	Lethal injection added in 1995, or electric chair; at inmate's option; by staff	Wisconsin	NA
		Wyoming	Lethal injection, unless held to be unconstitutional; gas then used; by outside person
South Dakota	Lethal injection, changed from electric chair in 1984; by undetermined source		
Tennessee	Lethal injection for offenses prior to 1-1-99; electric chair or lethal injection for offenses after 1-1-99, at inmate's option; by staff	Federal Bureau of Prisons	Lethal injection, unless for those cases covered under 18 U.S.C. 3596 that mandates method to be used as determined by the state in which the sentence was imposed
Texas	Lethal injection changed from electric chair; by staff		

Source: *Corrections Compendium*, September 1999.

The three-legged electric chair was constructed from oak by Department of Corrections personnel in 1998 and was installed at Florida State Prison in Starke in 1999. The previous chair was made by inmates from oak in 1923 after the Florida Legislature designated electrocution as the official mode of execution. (Prior to that, executions were carried out by counties, usually by hanging.) The apparatus that administers the electric current to the condemned inmate was not changed. It is regularly tested to ensure proper functioning (Florida Department of Corrections, 1999).

Other policies and procedures of concern to administrators include the following items, which have not been discussed previously.

- Timing and the process for separating inmates from others in the housing unit

- Moving an inmate from a housing facility to the execution unit
- Providing specifications for media access
- Establishing last meal regulations
- Timing for the inmates' "last statement," if one is allowed
- Dealing with communication of appeal possibilities
- Transporting inmates from the execution chamber to the place of internment
- Handling postexecution relations with the inmates' family and the media
- Debriefing of staff on the institutional impact of carrying out the capital punishment (see Chapter 4)
- Providing for relief of the pre- and postexecution trauma for staff

EXECUTIONER

Another key issue in developing policies and procedures for executions has been the assignment of the executioner. In the past, choices have ranged from anonymous members of the community to prison administrators. In Florida, the executioner is an anonymous private citizen who is paid $150 per execution. The position of excutiner was advertised in several Florida newspapers in 1978.

As in the case of counseling needs, there may be a special problem for those jurisdictions choosing an executioner from prison staff, especially in those cases where the staff has come to know the inmate over a prolonged period of time. Some wardens have argued that good policy dictates not assigning execution responsibilities to the same staff members who are responsible for the daily management of death-row inmates.

In some states that use lethal injection, a computer is used to randomly inject the lethal fluids that cause someone to die. The first state to use this method of lethal injection was Oklahoma, which adopted this procedure in 1977.

In advance of the execution, various syringes containing the following fluids are prepared to be administered at random or administered by the medical staff:

- 5.0 grams of sodium pentothal (which induces sleep)
- 50 cc of pancuronium bromide (which stops the breathing)
- 50 cc of potassium chloride (which stops the heart)

Additionally, attorneys will continue to watch these procedures closely for any legal improprieties that may save their clients at this last step in their lives. Also, the general public always has shown and continues to show an interest in this facet of prison administration, especially in those instances where either errors in the process or even lack of consistency can be discovered.

Finally, legal issues may affect some areas of these policies, such as the timing of the family notification or the number of witnesses. Legal issues may dictate a substantial portion of the policies and procedures that govern these and other issues.

WITNESSES

The number and type of witnesses at an execution will vary. In some jurisdictions, the penal code allows for members of the victim's family to be present, as well as a certain number of news media representatives. In some jurisdictions, as many as fifty individuals may witness an execution. The Missouri Penal Code specifies that the following individuals should be present:

- Warden
- Attorney general
- Reputable citizens (12)
- Physicians (2)
- Inmate's family/friends
- Inmate's spiritual adviser/chaplain

JUVENILES ON DEATH ROW

No other subgroup within the overall death-row population has received as much attention, both legal and public, as juveniles. Correctional administrators often face special issues with this group in both special needs programming and the frequent need for some level of separation of these young people from the rest of the population who have been given a death sentence. Most juveniles on death rows have become like those who are placed in protective custody within the general population of a prison.

In this country, more than 281 individuals were executed for crimes they committed under the age of eighteen, and at least 190 of them have been executed since 1900. A state corrections director has said that "by the time a 'youth' is to be executed, he has become an adult by any standard." This is especially so, if the average amount of time spent on a death row unit is now more than thirteen years. At the end of 1996, the Bureau of Justice Statistics reported that 2 percent of all the inmates placed on a death row in the United States were seventeen years old and younger. According to the Death Penalty Information Center, as of July 1999, there were seventy-four death row inmates sentenced as juveniles, and of this group, about 30 percent are in Texas. Thirteen men have been executed for crimes committed as juveniles since 1976. Questions about how to treat these young people can present administrators with difficult problems that are not likely to diminish.

In 1988, the U.S. Supreme Court ruled that the death penalty could not be imposed on anyone fifteen years of age or younger (*Thompson v. Okla-*

homa). A year later, the Supreme Court ruled that states were not banned from seeking the death penalty for those juveniles aged sixteen and seventeen. At that time, a minimum age of sixteen was established for the imposition of the death sentence.

Since then, due to the highly publicized cases of juveniles involved in multiple murders and mass shootings at schools and community centers throughout our nation, legislators have proposed laws that would allow the greater use of the death penalty for juveniles.

In Texas, a state legislator introduced a bill to make the state's justice system one of the strictest in the nation in its handling of the youngest of juvenile offenders. His proposal would reduce from the age of fourteen to ten, the age at which a youth can be tried in the adult criminal justice system and would allow juveniles as young as eleven to be charged with capital crimes and thus be eligible for execution. As of 1999, this legislation was still pending.

The philosophy that is emerging among these legislators is "if you do the crime, you will do the time." It also has brought on the need for the construction of correctional facilities to be used for young people who may be placed in a death-penalty situation. Many states are constructing facilities to house young people as low as the age of twelve who have committed capital crimes.

According to Amnesty International, the background of the majority of the juvenile offenders executed since 1990 was one of serious emotional or material deprivation. Many were regular users of drugs or alcohol with lower than average intelligence. Some had organic brain damage. Some had poor or inexperienced legal counsel. Highly relevant information was withheld at their trials due to incompetence or inexperience on the part of their lawyers. International human rights treaties prohibit anyone under eighteen years old at the time of the crime to be sentenced to death. The International Covenant on Civil and Political Rights, the American Convention on Human Rights, and United Nations Convention on the Rights of the Child all have provisions to this effect. More than 100 countries have laws specifically excluding the execution of child offenders (Juveniles and the Death Penalty: Executions Worldwide Since 1990, Amnesty International).

"The Juvenile Offenders and Victims Report of 1997" from the Office of Juvenile Justice and Delinquency Prevention notes that most juvenile death sentences eventually are reversed. Since 1973, 60 percent of these juvenile death sentences have been reversed, 6 percent have resulted in executions, and 34 percent are still in force. The majority of those juveniles who have been executed between January 1, 1973 and June 30, 1996 were Caucasian. Most of the sixty-four victims of the forty-eight inmates on death rows were adult victims between the ages of forty-two and sixty-four.

WOMEN ON DEATH ROW

As of April 1, 1999, fifty women were serving time on a death row in the United States (Death Penalty Information Center, 1999). This constitutes 1.4 percent of the total population of inmates who are currently on a death row in the United States.

Table 3.5 shows the accommodations for women on death row. Warden Jennie Lancaster explains the options and problems with housing this group of women:

> The typical housing configuration for women's facilities contain some type of segregation space, but these areas are designed to hold inmates who are restricted to cell time twenty-three hours daily. Consequently, the isolated death row inmate must endure similar restrictions, even though her behavior is acceptable" (Lancaster, 1991).

Some states house the female death-row inmate in the general population. However, this can lead to potential problems. First, the outside security perimeter is designed typically for medium-custody security practices. A death-row inmate could become an escape risk as the various legal processes continue on the case. Another potential problem relates to the needs most inmates have for developing relationships and close emotional bonds. These women identify with each other and express feelings in a verbal and physical manner (Lancaster, 1991). Lancaster reminds us (1991):

> It must be understood that many death-row inmates consider the women's prison to be home, and she is confident and comfortable with the staff in this emotionally charged time. The timing of her movement to another prison for death watch needs careful consideraton and planning by top agency managers.

In the months preceding Velma Barfield's execution date in North Carolina in 1984, many inmates in the population sought assistance from the staff to help manage their feelings related to Barfield's impending execution. These inmates had gotten to know Barfield when they were housed with her in the segregation unit, and the staff developed strategies to work with these women and the rest of the population. These circumstances might have been far more problematic if Barfield had been housed in the general population. The staff made structural changes in the segregation unit to provide her with significant out-of-cell time, but it still was inadequate (Lancaster, 1991).

In a 1997 survey (Salina and McCoy, 1999) of wardens in fourteen of the sixteen states that had women on a death row, the study found that death rows for women tended to become more "reformed" as more women inhabited

TABLE 3.5: FEMALE HOUSING ON DEATH ROW

States	Female Housing Breakdown	Physical Cell Accommodations
Alabama	1 separate facility	Individual cells
Alaska	NA	NA
Arizona	1 separate facility	Individual cells
Arkansas	1 woman housed at alternate unit	Individual cells
California	Women's prison	Individual cells
Colorado	NA	Individual cells
Connecticut	NA	Individual cells
Delaware	NA	Individual cells
D.C.	No Response	No Response
Florida	Separate facility	Individual cells
Georgia	No Response	No Response
Hawaii	NA	NA
Idaho	Women's prison	Individual cells
Illinois	1 separate facility	Individual cells
Indiana	1 separate facility	Individual cells
Iowa	NA	NA
Kansas	NA	Individual cells
Kentucky	NA	Individual cells
Louisiana	1 separate facility	Individual cells
Maine	NA	NA
Maryland	NA	Individual cells
Massachusetts	No Response	No Response
Michigan	NA	NA
Minnesota	NA	NA
Mississippi	1 separate facility	Individual cells
Missouri	No separate unit	2 per cell
Montana	NA	Individual cells
Nebraska	NA	Individual cells
Nevada	1 separate facility	Individual cells
New Hampshire	Same area as males	Single cells
New Jersey	Same area as males	Individual cells
New Mexico	NA	Individual cells
New York	Separate unit at female maximum security facility	Individual cells

States	Female Housing Breakdown	Physical Cell Accommodations
North Carolina	Women's prison	Individual cells
North Dakota	NA	NA
Ohio	NA	Individual cells
Oklahoma	Separate facility	Single or double; usually double
Oregon	NA	Individual cells
Pennsylvania	Separate facility	Individual cells
Rhode Island	NA	NA
South Carolina	NA	Individual cells
South Dakota	NA	Individual cells
Tennessee	Women's prison	Individual cells; double cells for women based on adapting to the system
Texas	Separate facility	Individual cells*
Utah	NA	Individual cells
Vermont	NA	NA
Virginia	NA	Individual cells
Washington	NA	Individual cells
West Virginia	NA	NA
Wisconsin	NA	NA
Wyoming	NA	Individual cells
Federal Bureau of Prisons	NA	Individual cells

*Updated November, 1999.
Source: *Corrections Compendium*, September 1999.

them. Restraint policies vary from no restraints to belly chains depending on where the death row is in relation to the rest of the prison.

In Florida, as in some other states, female death-row inmates are housed at a separate facility until immediately prior to their scheduled execution. At that time, female officers are provided by that facility to carry out the required security duties.

Female death-row inmates often require more personal attention because they tend to be quick to question any procedure or rule if they perceive that it is being unfairly applied to them in any way. Thus, staff must spend considerable time explaining procedures and reassuring the women that they are not being treated unfairly (Association of State Correctional Administrators, 1992).

However, according to Superintendent Mary Leftridge Byrd of the Pennsylvania Department of Corrections, Chester, Pennsylvania (ACA training seminar, 1999), it is important for wardens to examine the procedures and practices they use to be sure they truly are relevant to women and help the women maintain their dignity as individuals and do not simply use the procedures developed for men and hope that they fit the women. Women do have different needs and responses to them should be drafted by those who work with women. For example, consideration should be given to certain articles of clothing and personal care products. While these things may seem inconsequential in the grand scheme of things, they do add to the dignity of the individual.

Since 1976, three women have been executed in this nation: Velma Barfield in North Carolina, Judy Bueanoano in Florida, and Karla Faye Tucker in Texas. Perhaps the most notorious execution of a female offender has been Karla Faye Tucker. This probably was due to her spiritual commitment and her change during the time she had been incarcerated. Many special interest groups spoke out on her behalf, including Sister Helen Prejean, the author of the book *Dead Man Walking*, about an inmate on a death row.

One of the critical services for female death-row inmates is chaplaincy. Women on death row need consistent access to the chaplain. As the time on death row lengthens, the role of the chaplain becomes more of a stabilizing factor to the inmates and their families. In addition, the chaplain can select quality volunteers to provide services and support for these women. Chaplaincy should be a constant and stable venue for communication, which is an important aspect of managing female inmates (Lancaster, 1991). The visit and support of chaplaincy and counseling professionals for the benefit of the staff and other prisoners prior to an execution is of considerable importance, and helps to address individual staff concerns, and anxieties (Mary Leftridge Byrd, 1999).

In general, both the death-sentencing rate and the death-row population for women remain relatively small. Actual execution of female offenders is quite rare with only 533 documented executions since 1632. This number of female executions represents less than 3 percent of the total number of confirmed executions in the United States since the seventeenth century.

Since 1973, only 118 death sentences have been given to women, as compared to 6,302 death sentences that have been handed down to the entire population on death row. Of those, 118 death sentences handed down to these women, 72 of them have been reversed or commuted to life imprisonment (Bureau of Justice Statistics, 1998). Also, of the 118 death sentences that have been given to female offenders, only 43 of them are currently in effect. The states of Florida, North Carolina, and Texas account for nearly one-third of all such death sentences for women. The 48 women who are currently on a death row represent less than 0.1 percent of the approximately 63,000 women who are in prison in the United States.

As of 1998, the average female inmate on a death row was thirty-six years of age. The youngest was eighteen, and the oldest was seventy-four. Of these female inmates, 56 percent are white, 37 percent are black, and 7 percent are Hispanic.

Some of the main management challenges concern dealing with women in terms of different treatment of death row women, program parity with death row men, and the relationships with the media (Salinas and McCoy, 1999). Because there are so few women on most death rows, often the range of activities and programs for which they are eligible is quite limited.

PRESSURES FROM MEDIA, GOVERNMENT, AND SPECIAL INTEREST GROUPS

The administrators of death rows across the country receive a great deal of attention from the news media and certain public interest groups because of the nature of the final judgment of the death penalty. Therefore, it is important that each department of correction has a media policy that specifically describes what information will be released, who will have access to the inmate and at what times and with what limits, who on staff will be the spokesperson and relate the information, and in what form.

In 1992, Frank Hall, the director of the Oregon Department of Corrections told the Association of State Correctional Administrators (1992):

Death row inmates are allowed to contact the media and to be interviewed, photographed, and videotaped with their approval. Most are not anxious to have such contact, and our highest problem to date has been dealing with media who wanted to talk to death row inmates who did not want to talk to them.

In Florida, the media interest ebbs and flows (Association of State Correctional Administrators, 1992):

Initially, in 1979, with the resumption of executions, they were widely covered with satellite trucks as well as the print and voice media. However, with the execution in July 1992, there was not even one television satellite crew in the area.

In Nebraska, Harold Clarke, Director of the Department of Corrections states (Association of State Correctional Administrators, 1992):

Inmates must agree in writing to any media contact. Yet, as execution dates approach, the Department has had numerous media requests for interviews, photos, etc. [This is]time consuming for staff [and] tends to temporarily monopolize resources normally committed to facility operation.

The superintendent of the Indiana State Prison commented (Association of State Correctional Administrators, 1992):

It seems the media lack imagination since approximately 60 percent of all requests are related to capital punishment in some way. A few times, they have requested to interview offenders under the death sentence. The media are required to specify whom they wish to interview, and the requests are considered by the Superintendent with consultation at the Department level. Management problems have not occurred since the media are approved under the guidelines of who, what, when, where, why, and how. Once they agree to the guidelines, strict compliance occurs.

In California, media representatives cannot enter security housing units, condemned units, the gas chamber, or any area currently affected by an emergency situation without approval of the director or the director's designate. Another part of their policy states:

No camera or other recording device shall be permitted within the execution chamber area. Photographs or any other audio or visual recordings of an execution are prohibited. Media photography, filming, or video taping of the execution chamber is prohibited; however, stock department photographs and video tapes of the area are available upon request.

The Illinois Department of Corrections has the following policy on media interviews with death row inmates:

Section 103.40 News Media

A) Representatives of the media may be admitted to correctional facilities with approval of the Director. Access to facilities shall be limited to normal business hours whenever reasonable.
B) Requests for interviews with correctional employees shall be referred to the Director.
C) Face to face media interviews with committed persons under a sentence of death shall not be permitted unless personally authorized by the Director. Other media coverage may be allowed by the Director or his or her designee. All such deci-

sions shall be based upon, among other matters, the effect that an interview may have on the individual or other committed persons, and the effect upon safety, security, institutional order, or other penological concerns.

1. Media representatives may not photograph or interview a committed person without first obtaining his or her written consent, the written consent of his or her guardian if the committed person is under the age of 17, and the approval of the Director.
2. Members of the media may have access to committed persons under the same terms, conditions, and restrictions applicable to members of the general public.

D) Upon approval of a media request by the Director, the Director's office shall notify the Public Information Officer and the Deputy Director of the appropriate divisions.

(20 Illinois Administrative Code, effective July 1, 1996).

In Missouri:

Media visits to capital punishment inmates with a pending execution date will be processed as follows:

A. When the execution date is set by the Missouri Supreme Court, if there is insufficient time to accommodate all media requests, the department may consult with the inmate's attorney.
B. After the inmate is placed in a holding cell, media visits will not be permitted, and access will take place only by telephone.

(Missouri Department of Corrections, Public Information Procedure (7/08/96).

The following items are the relevant parts of the Texas Department of Criminal Justice's policy, ED-02.40 as of June 23, 1985.

"Procedures for News Media Interviews with Death Row Offenders

News media interviews of condemned prisoners are governed by the standards for interviewing specifically named offenders in Section V.D. below. Death row interviews shall be scheduled by the PIO and conducted at the Ellis Unit on Wednesdays and the Mountain View Unit on Thursdays for a period of two (2) hours. The Warden and the PIO shall determine the time period for the interviews. Any news media representatives requesting an interview with death row offenders should submit their names to the PIO prior to the announced interview date. Requests shall not be accepted at the unit of assignment. The number of offenders allowed to be interviewed shall be limited by the capacity of the interviewing area."

"Access by Other Writers and Researchers

Access to units/facilities and offender interviews for editorial researchers, independent film makers, writers for non-news magazines, and other non-news media representatives may be permitted by special advance arrangement and approval of the Warden on coordination with the PIO. Death row offender interviews and access to death row housing areas are not permitted during the week prior to a scheduled execution. Scholastic research requests should be made to Executive Services."

"Interviews with Specific Offenders

A news media reporter may interview a specifically named offender as arranged by prior appointment and with the written consent of the offender. An interview with a specifically named offender may be prohibited by the Warden, after consultation with the PIO, when the interview in the judgement of the Warden, would impair the rehabilitation of the offender; detract from the deterrence of crime; disrupt the safety and security of the unit/facility; or cause serious operations problems. In addition:

1. Interviews with offenders who are diagnosed with psychotic disorders are prohibited. Due to medical confidentiality laws, this reason shall not be cited.
2. An interview may be prohibited when the offender is in solitary confinement or administrative segregation.
3. An interview may be prohibited for a reasonable adjustment time (e.g., one [1] week) after the offender returns to prison on parole revocation.
4. If an offender is awaiting trial, such interviews may be permitted only with the consent of the offender's attorney, or if the offender does not have an attorney, with the consent of the court. If the Warden is not aware of the offender's status, he shall consult with the offender.
5. Each interview session shall not be more than 45 minutes in length."

It is also vital that clearly worded press releases provide information. It is often helpful to provide a chronology of people who have been executed by the state since the death penalty was reinstated. The following press releases from the North Carolina Department of Correction provide examples of the types of information that may be useful to provide. Note that the press release is run on the letterhead from the department and specifies that the contact person is the director of public information.

North Carolina Department of Correction
James B. Hunt, Jr., Governor
Theodis Beck, Secretary

Patty McQuillan, Director of Public Information
(919) 733-4926
July 30, 1999

WITNESS SELECTED FOR AUGUST 6 EXECUTION

Raleigh Central Prison. Warden R. C. Lee named six official witnesses and five media witnesses for the Aug. 6 execution of Joseph Timothy Keel.

The official witnesses selected by the District Attorney's office in the Seventh Prosecutorial District are: Mack Daniel Simmons, Jr., Linda Jean S. Moore, Jennifer Simmons Becknell, and Bobby Dale Smith. The two media witnesses from the Edgecombe County Sheriff's Department are Lt. Jerry Wiggs and Sgt. Donald Lynn.

Media witnesses are Connie Rhem of *The Wilson Daily Times* in Wilson, Thomas McDonald of *The Daily Southerner* in Tarboro, Mark Roberts from WRAL-TV in Raleigh, Steve Adams from WEEB Radio in Southern Pines, and Estes Thompson from the Associated Press.

Keel is scheduled to be executed at Central Prison at 2 A.M. , Fri., Aug. 6 by lethal injection. Edgecombe Superior Court sentenced Keel to death on March 30, 1993 for the murder of his father-in-law, John Simmons, on July 10, 1990.

Under Department of Correction policy, the district attorney and sheriff in the county of conviction nominate the six official witnesses. These witnesses may include members of the victim's family. A 1997 amendment to the state statute ensures the crime victim's family the right to witness the execution.

The Radio Television News Directors Association of the Carolinas selected the broadcast reporters and the N. C. Press Association selected the two print reporters. The Associated Press selects its own wire service representative. Following the execution, the media witnesses are required to relate their experience to other reporters immediately in Central Prison's visitor center.

Twelve people have been executed since 1977 when the death penalty was reinstated:

James W. Hutchins of McDowell County was executed March 16, 1984.

Velma M. Barfield of Balden County was executed on Nov. 2, 1984.

John W. Rook of Wake County was executed on Sept. 19, 1986.

Michael V. McDougall of Mecklenburg County was executed on
    Oct. 18, 1991.

John S. Gardner Jr. of Forsyth County was executed on Oct. 23, 1992.
David Lawson of Cabarrus County was executed on June 15, 1994.
Kermit Smith of Halifax County was executed on Jan. 24, 1995.
Phillip Ingle of Rutherford County was executed on Sept. 22, 1995.
Ricky L. Sanderson of Iredell County was executed on Jan. 30, 1998.
Zane B. Hill of Buncombe County was executed on Aug. 14, 1998.
John T. Noland of Mecklenburg County was executed on Nov. 20, 1998.
James David Rich of Greene County was executed on March 26, 1999.

North Carolina Department of Correction
Keel Execution Media Advisory

Monday, Aug. 2, 1999

Death row inmate Joseph Timothy Keel is scheduled for execution Friday, Aug. 6, 1999, at 2 A.M. at Central Prison in Raleigh. Keel was convicted March 30, 1993, in Edgecombe Superior Court for the murder of his father-in-law, John Simmons, July 10, 1990.

Media who need to photograph the death watch area and the execution chamber in Central Prison may do so Monday, Aug. 2, at 10 A.M. Cameras and tape recorders are allowed. *This will be the only time news media will be allowed into the execution chamber before the execution.*

Newspaper, television and radio reporters and photographers should be at Central Prison's visitor center promptly at 10 A.M. Media should bring a photo I.D. and media identification. Warden R. C. Lee will explain execution procedures. The session will last one hour.

Reporters who plan to attend should call the Department of Correction Public Information Office at (919) 733-4926.

Joseph Timothy Keel is among 197 inmates on death row. Requests for media interviews must go through attorneys Jay Ferguson or Brian Aus, 919-682-5648. Their fax # is 919-688-7251.

Television programs, such as *Nightline, Justice Files,* and other documentaries have discussed whether the use of the death penalty is a deterrent to crime. Many of these types of programs have reported the executions of various individual inmates. Most of the time, the media sensationalizes such events. Because of this, some institutions have grappled with the problem of crowd control by setting aside an area outside the secure perimeter for parking and those standing by, when an execution is taking place.

As the general interest of the public rises on this issue, most administrators have been faced with the need to set aside an outside parking area, outside of the secure perimeter, to handle parking of large television-production vehicles and the presence of news media and special interest groups when an execution is about to take place. Administrators have had to write special policies and procedures to handle the large number of people who are involved in the reporting of the news and the protests of special interest groups who may be conducting midnight candlelight vigils and other protests.

Training seminars at the National Institute of Corrections address the elements that should be in a good press-release package when an execution is going to take place. The National Institute of Corrections also recommended the following items:

- Select and train several high-ranking staff to be coordinators with the media both long before and during the execution.
- Select reasonable accommodations for print, video, and radio media at the selected site for the press.
- Give the press the do's and don't's ahead of time.
- Remind staff far ahead of the actual execution of the policy of the correctional department and the institution regarding talking with the press, and remind staff not to give personal comments.
- Make decisions about press access to the inmate and coordinate this with the inmate's attorney.

Many prison administrators are exposed to the various shifts in correctional philosophy emanating from the legislative and executive branches of the state and federal government. In 1996, President Bill Clinton signed a crime bill making dozens of federal crimes subject to the death penalty. While correctional administrators have little or no control over such shifts in thinking and action, correctional managers and administrators must deal with the consequences of such shifts on a daily basis.

The National Institute of Corrections' training suggests that wardens expect "political" interference by various interest groups, legislators, and the governor's office. They warn that often these groups can cause confusion at the last minute. For example, in one state the governor made some statements about organ donation that were contrary to state correctional policy.

Changes in political leadership often are accompanied by changes in philosophy about the use of the death penalty. In several cases, incoming governors have reversed their predecessor's position either for or against conducting executions. In March of 1995, the Governor of New York signed a new death penalty law updating the use of New York's death penalty and procedures. In a Gallup poll, which was taken shortly after the law was passed, most New Yorkers favored life sentences over the death penalty for first-degree murder. Forty-four percent opted for a life sentence without parole; 38 percent chose the death penalty, and 9 percent preferred life with a chance of parole as an appropriate sentence. With the lack of a consistent point of view and inconsistent expectations, new pressures are focused on the death-row unit and those administrators and staff who are charged with carrying out the death penalty.

PUBLIC OPINION ON CAPITAL PUNISHMENT

Gallup polls reveal the concerns of the general public and also affect those who are in correctional management of death-row units. A Gallup poll of January 1989, which was issued in a copy of *U.S. News and World Report*, showed that 79 percent of Americans support the use of capital punishment, which was an increase over the 42 percent that was reported in 1966. However, the readers of this magazine may not reflect a national consensus and the placement of the poll in this particular magazine may have skewed the results.

In a Gallup poll of May 1995, reported in the August 14, 1995 *Christianity Today*, 77 percent of Americans supported the use of the death penalty while only 13 percent opposed it, with the remaining 10 percent undecided. According to this survey, 89 percent of Republicans favor the death penalty, while Democrats support the death penalty by a margin of 67 percent to 20 percent. And despite claims of bias, according to the survey results, 55 percent of black Protestants support capital punishment while 30 percent oppose it. Again, the placement of the poll in this particular publication may have skewed the results.

According to a survey of the former and present presidents of the country's top academic criminological societies, 84 percent rejected the notion that the death penalty acts as a deterrent to murder (quoted in Death Penalty Information Center, 1999; survey by Radelet and Akers, 1996). If the death penalty were a deterrant, then the south, with the highest murder rate of any section of the country, would not account for 80 percent of all executions.

Since that time, an increasing number of Americans support the use of alternatives to the death penalty and as Chart 3.1 illustrates more police chiefs across the nation place the use of the death penalty last as a way to reduce violent crime (Death Penalty Information Center, 1999). Almost a third of police chiefs state that reducing drug abuse is a way to reduce violent crime. Fifteen percent throw the ball into the corrections court and suggest longer prison sentences as a way to reduce violent crime.

In fact, public support for the death penalty drops to below 50 percent when voters are offered alternative sentences. More people would support life without parole plus restitution to the victim's family than would choose the death penalty (Death Penalty Information Center, 1999).

CHART 3.1: POLICE CHIEF'S RATINGS OF WAYS TO REDUCE VIOLENT CRIME

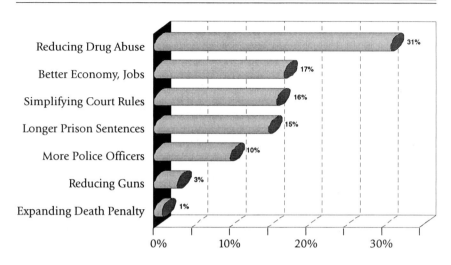

Reducing Drug Abuse — 31%
Better Economy, Jobs — 17%
Simplifying Court Rules — 16%
Longer Prison Sentences — 15%
More Police Officers — 10%
Reducing Guns — 3%
Expanding Death Penalty — 1%

Source: *Death Penalty Information Center*, 1999 based on 1995 Hart Research Poll

INTERNATIONAL CONCERNS

Worldwide, the United Nations Commission on Human Rights renewed its call for a worldwide moratorium on executions. Resolution 61 states that "the Commission calls upon all states that still maintain the death penalty to establish a moratorium on executions with a view to completely abolishing the death penalty."

The resolution specifically asks states not to impose the punishment "for nonviolent financial crimes or for nonviolent religious practice or expression of conscience," nor to "impose the death penalty on a person suffering from any form of mental disorder." This resolution received the support from seventy-two cosponsoring countries.

Meanwhile, the United Nations Special Rapporteur issued a report that states "the death penalty should under no circumstances be mandatory by law, regardless of the changes involved." Interestingly, in 1999, acting on the recommendation of the Presidential Clemency Commission Chairman Anatoly Pristavkin, Russian Federation President Boris Yeltsin commuted all 716 death sentences outstanding. And following a ruling of the constitutional court, no further death sentences can be imposed until the constitutional requirement for trial by jury in capital cases can be met in all eighty-nine regions of the Federation.

In American Samoa, Governor Tauese Sunia has refused to sign legislation proposing lethal injection as the means of execution on the island. Although the Samoan penal code allows the death penalty for murder, there have been no executions since the 1920s. Governor Tauese said, "I am against killing people. It doesn't correct the crime that was committed and the taking of a life at any time doesn't make it right," according to *Death Penalty News, June 1999* .

In the Philippines, according to Amnesty International, since the reintroduction of the death penalty in 1993, the Philippines has gone from an abolitionist position to having one of the highest death-sentencing rates in the world. More than 900 people convicted of capital offenses are now under a sentence of death.

In the United States, according to Amnesty International, there are more than seventy foreign nationals under sentence of death, many of whom have not been made aware of their rights under the Vienna Convention, to which the United States is a signatory. Cases are expected to be brought before the International Court of Justice.

CHAPTER 4

MANAGEMENT PRACTICES AND OPTIONS

Perhaps more than any other classification of inmates, those in a correctional center or prison with a death sentence present both changing and specialized management challenges to correctional officers who oversee them. Managing death-sentenced inmates consumes a relatively high percentage of administrative time and energy. This is especially true when one considers the legal scrutiny, public awareness and interest, the increased security concerns, and the transportation and visitation difficulties of managing such individuals.

PERSONNEL ADMINISTRATION

Nearly every department of corrections or institution which houses death-sentenced inmates has a written policy that includes the listing of the different personnel involved in the various levels of administration, along with a description of their duties, responsibilities, and job assignments. These policies include details for staff members directly involved in the daily operation of the unit or units where death-sentenced inmates are housed, and also include details for those staff members who primarily are involved in the administrative management of such inmates. The policies provide a description of the roles and responsibilities for each of these staff members. In jurisdictions without specific litigation, such policies often include specific functions within the institution. For example, a job description that states, "The warden will visit the unit at least every two weeks" may prevent court involvement in their policy making.

Traditional line staff, including security personnel, transportation staff, and their immediate supervisors, often have job descriptions that apply to their role on death-row units. In many cases, these assignments include clearly defined lines of authority and chain-of-command obligations, detailing operations such as the keeping of a logbook and its various entries, visual inspections, use-of-force guidelines, work and shift schedules, and similar operational procedures related to managing this group of inmates. The ever-present legal scrutiny over death-row units over the past two decades may be part of the motivation for defining these roles and seeing that these roles are carried out properly.

STAFFING

Staffing was reported to be a problem in eleven states in 1992 (*Corrections Compendium*, 1992). There was not enough staff to fully carry out all programming—from exercise to showers. Security depends on staffing.

A National Institute of Corrections' seminar warns, "You may find staff facing the irony of choosing to work in this business to help change people's lives and now, after taking care of an inmate for ten years they are asked to methodically plan and complete the process of an execution."

The staff will receive many questions from their families, neighbors, church members, and others. The stress from these issues can make staff feel isolated, and they will turn to their peers for support. The family also becomes isolated. Counseling needs to address the questions of what to tell these individuals to help prepare them for the inevitable questions.

A National Institute of Corrections' seminar suggested several procedures for selecting staff who will be involved in the actual execution. They recommend "Identify the key staff roles that must be present during the death watch time, execution preparation, and actual execution." They further suggest, "be clear about their roles and interview staff. The issues must be honestly presented and any personal staff issues should be respected. The warden should stay in some kind of contact with key personnel." The seminar warns, "expect some to 'dropout' as actual simulations begin to occur."

The issue of confidentiality must be clear in all operations. It should be part of the standard operating procedures that the behavior of the staff is professional and any deviation from this standard will not be tolerated.

Consider using staff in the death watch area who have not been involved in managing the condemned inmate for any significant period of time. An important management issue that many employees have confronted is that the same employees who must manage death-row inmates are also the same employees who must execute the death-row inmate. This situation is extremely difficult for both the inmate and the employee (Association of State Correctional Administrators, 1992).

In Wyoming, staff assigned to the death row do receive special training at both a formal and informal, on-the-job, level. Formal training includes death house management, which is contained in an eighty-hour segment. Training generally consists of the strategies necessary to manage an inmate for a long duration in an intense maximum-security environment.

Staff Training

All of the states reporting had written policies and procedures in place for an execution. Several states even have made a video of the execution protocol, and use this video as a training tool for the execution team. Many states and jurisdictions have included the use of "walk-throughs" of the procedures that are to be followed in the event of an execution. Such training is important because an execution is a very sobering experience for both line staff and administrators, especially when they have not been involved in an execution before.

The execution of an inmate is one of the most serious responsibilities assigned to the department of corrections and the individual institution. An execution generates a great deal of public debate and attention and is a time for all staff to be aware of the pressures on themselves and other staff and the extra security precautions that are necessary.

Many jurisdictions reported their need for specialized training for their staff and for counseling services to be available both to their staff and inmates as a part of the overall procedures of the execution process. This need appears to be connected with the longer appeals process, which is now common, and consequently, the longer stays during which inmates and staff come to know each other. In these situations, the correctional staff get to know the inmate, and, in many cases, have known this person for several years, so the loss of this individual causes the staff some trauma for which they may need some counseling.

In jurisdictions where an execution has not been conducted, it is apparent that walk-throughs and the use of protocol videos are very important parts of the staff and management training. This is true, especially where there is an opportunity for staff and administrators to discuss their reactions in some depth after the execution has been completed. Such an exercise also is helpful and should lead to a review of policies and procedures to see if any changes might be desirable.

In Wyoming, employees receive information relative to escort, cell searches, mail, food service, medications, records, management, observation of behavior, emergency procedures, pre-execution management, execution management, and general relationship with the death house inmate (Association of State Correctional Administrators, 1992).

Employees who may exhibit vulnerability and/or who may tend to over identify with a death house inmate are not assigned to the death house.

Employees always manage the death house as a team of not less than two employees, preferably, three (Association of State Correctional Administrators, 1992).

In South Carolina, on-the-job training is provided and there are monthly and other periodic briefings among the staff regarding their responsibilities in the unit. Specialized training relative to how to deal with disruptive persons and other appropriate issues is provided to employees in death row and all lockup areas of the department (Association of State Correctional Administrators, 1992).

In Nevada, correctional officer trainees (those with less than one year of experience) are not assigned to work in death row units unless under direct supervision (Association of State Correctional Administrators, 1992).

In Florida, there are no special training programs to prepare staff to work with death-row inmates. Rather, they must meet the minimum standards for a correctional officer. Once hired, they are observed in a progression of duties, and the observations of supervisors and fellow officers help identify staff that would be amenable to working with this select group of inmates. At that point, on-the-job training with a seasoned officer is used as the main training mode (Association of State Correctional Administrators, 1992).

It is important for correctional administrators to consider the stress placed on the administration, including the staff and families of those who work in facilities with death-row units. Training and debriefing for the staff may be very useful.

SOME STATE EXAMPLES

Housing and Classification

Some of the main issues that correctional administrators have within their control include whether offenders live in the population or are segregated in their own death-row unit. Then, within this there is the issue of classification of these inmates.

Mainstreaming

In the capital punishment section in Potosi, Missouri, in 1989, the inmates were divided into minimum, medium, and administrative segregation. The facility had two distinct and separate operations—those for capital punishment inmates and those for noncapital punishment inmates. The institutional time schedule was divided between general population and capital punishment inmates. Capital punishment inmates were moved by escort and in restraints. The recreation, dining room, and other facilities were not shared. Job assignments for capital punishment inmates were limited to their housing unit. By 1990, the administrators decided to mainstream the inmates. This freed up a number of beds and eliminated the dual-service delivery system. It reduced and simplified litigation dealing with unequal treatment. It simplified staff scheduling. The actual go-ahead to mainstream occurred in 1991.

The advantages of mainstreaming included the following:
- Canteen hours were expanded.
- Psychological services were available for the entire population on a more informal basis with more services available to all inmates.
- Joint recreation and hobby craft periods made more time available for all.
- Capital punishment inmates no longer were escorted or in restraints while in movement.
- There was a big gain in health care services for the entire population. Capital punishment inmates no longer had to wait to be escorted to medical call. Physicians no longer were required to go to the capital punishment unit. More physician time was then available to all inmates.
- Visiting privileges were greatly enhanced. All population based on their security classification have full or limited contact visits.
- Staff services were more equitably distributed.
- Posts were reassigned to enhance total security.
- All institutional jobs were available to the entire inmate population.

The problems of separating inmates with a pending execution date are handled on a case-by-case basis, sometimes only three days prior to execution. After three years, the administrators report "staff is fully committed to the concept [mainstreaming capital punishment inmates] and would not want to return to the old ways."

Florida's Daily Routine for Death Row Inmates

On their webpage, Florida provides information on their death penalty. The following description of the daily routine of death-row inmates provides administrators with a description of how Florida manages this group.

The Daily Routine for Death-row Inmates

DEATH-ROW AND DEATH-WATCH CELLS

A death-row cell is 6 x 9 x 9.5 feet high. Florida State Prison also has death-watch cells to incarcerate inmates awaiting execution after the Governor signs a death warrant for them. A death-watch cell is 12 x 7 x 8.5 feet high.

Meals

Death-row inmates are served meals three times a day: at 5:00 A.M. from 10:30 A.M. to 11:00 A.M., and from 4:00 P.M. to 4:30 P.M. Food is prepared by FSP personnel and is transported in insulated carts to the cells. Inmates are allowed plates and spoons to eat their meals. Prior to execution, an inmate may request a last meal. To avoid extravagance, the food to prepare the last meal must cost no more than $20 and must be purchased locally.

Visitors

Visitors are allowed every weekend from 9 A.M. to 3 P.M. All visitors must be approved by prison officials before being placed on the inmate visitor list. Visitors traveling over 200 miles may visit both Saturday and Sunday. Members of the news media may request death-row inmate interviews through the Department of Corrections public affairs office at (850) 488-0420. Inmates must agree to being interviewed. Because of safety and security concerns, the news media may not interview any prison personnel who are involved in executions except for official Department of Corrections spokesman.

Showers

The inmates may shower every other day.

Security

Death-row inmates are counted at least once an hour. They are escorted in handcuffs and wear them everywhere except in their cells, the exercise yard, and the shower. They are in their cells at all times except for medical reasons, exercise, social or legal visits, or media interviews. When a death warrant is signed, the inmate is put under death watch status and is allowed a legal and social phone call.

Mail, Magazines, and Entertainment

Inmates may receive mail every day except holidays and weekends. They may have cigarettes, snacks, radios, and black and white televisions in their cells. They do not have cable television or air conditioning, and they are not allowed to be with each other in a common room. They can watch church services on closed-circuit television. While on death watch, inmates may have radios and black and white televisions positioned outside their cell bars.

Clothing

Death-row inmates can be distinguished from other inmates by their orange T-shirts. Their pants are the same blue colored pants worn by regular inmates.

Cost

It costs approximately $55.14 per day to incarcerate a death-row inmate.

Tennessee's Timetable

Tennessee was under court order to develop a better procedure and housing for its death-row inmates. So, in 1989, the state named a unit manager to run the death-row component. This person implemented, organized, and trained staff on the operational and programmatic procedures that would be used. The new death-row unit opened in October 1989 with a staff that had been trained completely in the operational procedures of the unit. Staff had been carefully screened and advised of the problems associated with dealing with those inmates with a death sentence.

Other than supervisors, a large percentage of the staff who opened the death row unit had less than six months of correctional experience. The movement to the new location and the implementation of security and programmatic needs was placed into effect immediately. The implementation process went without major problems, but the adjustment of those inmates occupying a new housing unit became quite extensive. Those assigned to different pods within the unit were isolated from friends or associates they had lived with for many years; even correctional officers who were assigned to different pods had limited contact with those inmates. Although the death-row inmates had been responsible for a class action suit based on the conditions of the old death-row unit, they began to wish that they were at their old location.

Again, change became the major problem. By early 1990, the inmates and staff had settled into an operation that created an atmosphere that had never been felt in a death row before. The unit is fully programmed for those inmates who exhibit appropriate behavior and who want to work and enjoy the freedom associated with their programs. The unit also has those inmates who are confined to their cells twenty-three hours a day and escorted in full restraints by two correctional officers during any movement. The problems associated with the existing unit have been very limited. The death-row unit in Tennessee at this time has been praised by correctional people through the country and from foreign lands. Documentaries have been made concerning the programs, and now plans are being made for possible expansion of the program in the future, according to *Management of Death Row* (93-P2601, March 14-19, 1993) available from the National Institute of Corrections.

The time line on page 78, which was developed to meet the court order, may be useful for other administrators as one way to examine their death-row units. The first step may be to see if these things are in place, and if not, to establish a time line for their completion. Administrators who are using this time line may wish to add other elements to it to meet the needs that they have. Then, each of the main ideas on it may be broken down into detailed tasks, each with its own date for completion.

Time Line for Instituting Changes in Tennessees' Death-row Unit

Establish privilege levels based on inmates' behavior.

Appoint a program director.

Provide intensive training of officers assigned to a death row unit in the following areas:
- Policies and procedures
- Post orders
- Stress management
- Interpersonal skills of communication

This training participation will be by officers during their off-duty time without overtime compensation, to which many officers objected. There is also ongoing training with regular/relief officers.

Maintain a regular supervisor and supervisor relief.

Develop a system for consistent enforcement of security regulations.

Install a TV monitoring system and intercom on all walks for communication with the front lobby.

Develop a food services program.
- Weekly group dinners for designated levels.
- Assign level 1 inmates to maintain sanitation of food service line and to deliver food to inmates. [The food is the same as that served to the general population. On a daily basis, monitor the proper temperature on food so that it is maintained.]

Develop a program for religious services.
- Chaplain to provide individual religious counseling and crisis counseling, as needed, and individual religious study courses, on request.
- Chaplain holds level 1 and 2 group religious services (weekly).
- Chaplain coordinates the free world religious visits.

Develop a plan for education services.
- Provide level 1 and 2 group classes.
- Provide level 3 and 4 access to individual education/instruction in their cell on a regularly scheduled basis.
- Provide special education.
- Provide adult basic education and general equivalency degree study (as of March 1, 1988, eleven inmates had received their GED).

Develop policies and procedures for the commissary.

- All levels may receive a weekly order in approved containers. [Items classified as security risks shall be omitted.]

Arrange process for medical issues.

- Provide access to the daily sick call. A medical practitioner is to conduct triage at the cell. There is an opportunity to seek medical assistance at a given time.

Schedule exercise and out-of-cell activity.

- Construct new exercise area and install new equipment and telephones.
- Permit level 1 inmates to have access to a group exercise yard in which they can engage in team and dual sports, have telephone privileges, and the opportunity to interact socially.
- Allow level 1 group/team sports, card and domino games inside during bad weather.
- Permit level 2 group exercises in any exercise area except a large yard.
- Provide level 3 and 4 individual exercise yards, where three universal gyms have been installed.

Develop plan for art and crafts.

- Plan program space construction. Inmates at all levels must purchase arts and crafts supplies to produce art work. All items must meet security approval.

Arrange for group and individual counseling.

- There is a permanently assigned full-time counselor for the death row.
- Counseling is provided to all inmates. Individual counseling is held on a weekly basis. Group counseling to levels 1 and 2 occurs on a regularly scheduled basis. Initially, there was a lack of staff and a lack of interest by inmates, but this has been resolved.

Develop a system to meet proper sanitation and environmental conditions.

- Improve pest control (spray monthly). Initially, inmates refused to have their cells sprayed.
- Inspect cells weekly. Initially, there was a lack of time due to other program needs, but eventually, this was implemented and is conducted weekly.

Examine procedures on fire safety.

- Provide heaters on the walk.

- Conduct quarterly fire drills (simulated) in conjunction with normal movements. There is an inability to release all inmates during fire drills.
- Conduct fire drills for officers on a quarterly basis.
- Orient new officers to fire safety procedures when they assume their duties in the unit.
- Purchase a Scott Air pack.

Improve Inmate-Staff Communication.
- Conduct monthly community meetings with the warden and an inmate representative.
- Establish a grievance procedure internal to Unit VI.

Jobs.
- Establish and assign inmate jobs for level 1 and 2 to the twenty-three jobs available. Problems incurred in establishing these jobs include: out-of-cell time to work, staff involvement, staff understanding of their role, and security acceptance of jobs. For various reasons, the following jobs were abolished: one maintenance person, a counselor's aide, a pest control person, and leather goods person; the following were added: arts and crafts instructor (two), exercise equipment maintenance person, one painter, and one legal aide.

- Jobs include the following:
  — Law library and custodian (legal aide)
  — Barber (two)
  — Painter
  — Maintenance
  — Laundry custodian
  — Tutor (teacher aide)
  — Custodian—exercise area
  — Rock men (four)
  — Clerk typist (law material)
  — Counselor's aide
  — Pest control
  — Food service (two)

Establish a new law library.
- Legal materials are to be available in a law library within the unit that is staffed by a level 1 inmate assistant. Initially, there was an overload of requests to use available space, but subsequently, area bookshelves were expanded and stocked. There is a complete set of

new law books and related material.

- The use of a headphone is required for audio equipment such as televisions and radios. The problems incurred in this were a lack of qualified installers, a lack of parts to install jacks, and the fact that the headsets are easily broken. The jacks and the headsets are replaced, as needed.

Renovate visitation rooms to accommodate additional visitors.

Build new death-row unit at new prison.

TIMING: MIDNIGHT OR DAYLIGHT

In most states, an execution is conducted at midnight to preserve the entire twenty-four-hour period of an execution warrant. If a last minute stay of execution is not granted, the state would be able to carry out the execution on the date of the Supreme Court's warrant. North Carolina executes its prisoners at 2:00 A.M. so that both the public and the inmate population will be more sedate and controlled.

Although midnight executions are beneficial to prison management because the entire inmate population is locked down for the night, other issues concern the availability of witnesses and state officials, and various judges who would have to be awakened late at night or in the early morning hours to hear arguments for or against a stay of execution. In May 1998, Arizona scheduled its first execution during the daytime hours.

A RELEVANT ACA STANDARD

Although death-sentenced inmates generally are not considered to be in administrative segregation or protective custody, a correctional standard of the American Correctional Association in *Adult Correctional Institutions,* Third Edition, concerning programs and services for this group may provide guidance on the programming and services that should be provided to death-sentenced inmates.

ACA STANDARD 3-4261

Written policy, procedure and practice provide that inmates in administrative segregation and protective custody have access to programs and services that include, but are not limited to, the following: educational services, commissary services, library services, social services, counseling services, religious guidance, and recreational programs.

DISCUSSION: Although services and programs cannot be identical to those provided to the general population, there should be no major differences for reasons other than danger to life, health, or safety. Inmates in administrative segregation and protective custody should have the opportunity to receive treatment from professionals, such as social service workers, psychologists, counselors and psychiatrists. The standard also applies to inmates held in disciplinary detention for more than sixty days.

EXECUTING THE INNOCENT

Since 1970, more than seventy-four people were released from death-row units across the United States because they were able to gain new evidence of their innocence. In the *Chicago Sun Times* of June 15, 1996, staff reporter Lee Bey reported that four men were released from the death-row unit in Illinois. One of those men, Dennis (Buck) Williams, had served eighteen years on the death-row unit before he was released. Due to the work of three Northwestern University students, Dennis Williams was given an opportunity to show the courts his innocence and prove his wrongful death-penalty sentence. Because there is room for error and the possibility of a change in an inmate's status, it is important to consider programming and services for such inmates. In this case, special credit goes to the chaplain and volunteers who faithfully ministered to Dennis Williams on the death-row gallery, and to those staff members who helped him keep his sanity during his long ordeal.

COST: BUDGET CONCERNS

The cost of actually putting someone to death has risen over the past two decades. In the 1930s, when someone was executed by hanging, the cost was very nominal because the most expensive budget items were the purchase of a new rope and the fee for the hangman.

However, at the present time, executing someone by lethal injection costs more than 3.5 million dollars. The actual cost of the syringes and lethal solutions that are used in this style of execution is only about $346.17; the cost of defending appeals of a death-sentenced inmate brings the cost into millions of dollars.

In July of 1988, the *Miami Herald* reported that Florida spent an estimated $57 million on the death penalty from 1973 to 1988 to put eighteen inmates to death. This is an average of $3.2 million spent per execution.

One of the states that employs the lethal-injection method has constructed a facility that houses a double death chamber to cut down on the cost and expenses of performing an execution. The idea here is that you would have to pay the execution team only once for that day's work. The old saying of "buy one, get one free" sticks in one's mind as you think of this move to cut the cost of such executions.

In May of 1993, Duke University conducted a comprehensive study which showed that the one completed death penalty in North Carolina cost the state $2.16 million more than the cost of putting someone in prison for life. On a national basis, these figures translate to an extra cost of more than $900 million spent since the reinstitution of the death penalty in 1976.

In March of 1988, the *Sacramento Bee* reported that the state of California spent more than $90 million annually beyond the ordinary cost of the California justice system. Of this total, $78 million was incurred at the trial level.

In March of 1992, the *Dallas Morning Herald* reported that in Texas, a death penalty case cost an average of $2.3 million. This is approximately three times more than the cost of imprisoning someone in a single cell at the highest security level for forty years.

Throughout the country, at the highest level of security, it would cost approximately $800,000 to $1 million to put someone in prison for life. Contrast this with the approximately $2.3 million for an execution.

Most recently, a death-row inmate who was released from prison because of DNA testing brought suit against that state because of his incarceration and won a settlement of more than seven million dollars. This figure, along with the cost of his incarceration on a death-row unit for several years, amounts to approximately 10 million dollars.

The question that arises is, where are the funds going to come from to continue to pay for future executions? If the costs are in the millions of dollars now, what will the costs be in the future?

SUMMARY AND CONCLUSIONS

Our study confirms the assumption that inmates under the sentence of death present a very unique set of correctional management concerns.

1. *Increasing Time Served on Death Row*—The existence of death rows where inmates remain for extremely long periods of time due to the uncertainty of the outcome of their sentence is a continually growing phenomenon in American corrections. Before 1976, the average time served on a death row was thirteen months. As of 1998, that time had stretched to thirteen or fourteen years.
2. *The Number of Death-sentenced Inmates Vary*—The size of death-sentenced populations varies considerably from jurisdiction to jurisdiction and from institution to institution. Some jurisdictions have less than 10 death-sentenced inmates and a few have more than 300 death-sentenced inmates.

Managing a death-sentenced population of more than 100 inmates continues to present management problems and challenges.

3. *Isolation from or Mixture with General Population*—A critical management issue is whether to isolate or segregate inmates with death sentences from the general prison populations, or by using a classification process, identify those inmates who could be managed in the general prison population. In most institutions, the housing and programming for inmates with death sentences are dictated by the sentence itself; that is, once a person receives a death sentence, he or she is subject to the particular housing, programs, privileges, physical restraints, and so forth, that are accorded to all inmates with a death sentence in that institution.

4. *Public and Political Controversy*—Because of the ever-increasing public awareness of the use of the death penalty due to media attention, the use of the Internet, and the outcry of various special interest groups, administrators are under intense public scrutiny. Couple this with the focus of political candidates who use death penalty issues, and it is easy to understand the stress of persons responsible for carrying out the laws of the nation and states. Such scrutiny requires that much time and energy must be devoted to the "public relations" aspect of managing death-row inmates.

5. *Staffing*—With the growing numbers of inmates with a death-row status and the scrutiny they receive, it is very important that there be a full staffing complement for such units. Training for this staff is critical, so they can avoid the problems recently witnessed in Florida when a death-row inmate who had killed a correctional officer was allegedly beaten to death by correctional officers. The professional responsibilities and stress of working closely with people who are under the sentence of death for longer periods of time differ significantly from the stresses found in other correctional staff assignments. Yet, staff who work closely with inmates who are under the sentence of death receive no specialized training for this assignment beyond their training in security procedures. The desirability of special training in such areas as stress management, legal issues, and counseling have been raised by administrators, staff, and inmates. Along with this training, several experts have suggested increased compensation for those officers and staff who work on death-row units

6. *Programming*—In general, inmates who are serving time under the sentence of death have very limited access to programs. Whether this is for punitive reasons or not, the need for constructive activities (for example, physical recreation, work therapy, and religious programs) both to pass the time and to relieve tension was cited by staff and inmates alike. Opportunities to be able to communicate with family and friends, either by telephone or in person, assume great importance for inmates in this

status. Visitation policies and procedures seem to vary widely among institutions. According to staff who work with death-sentenced inmates, there is a need for adequate access by inmates under sentences of death to legal assistance (a law library and attorneys) and counseling services (religious and psychological).

7. *Cost Factor*—With a growing population of death-sentenced inmates, the costs of housing, programming, counseling services, legal defenses, and so forth, are growing as well. Because of this cost factor, officials should expect increased efforts to provide alternatives to the death sentence.

8. *Juvenile Death Sentences*—With the massacre at Columbine High School in mind, and despite the decline in violent crime among juveniles, we can expect a growing number of juveniles to be sentenced to death-row units. These youths are difficult to manage in any facility but may be a major challenge to this unit where they will gain their maturity as they await their final sentence. Staff who work with these youths will need specialized training to be able to manage such inmates.

AFTERTHOUGHTS

In looking back over the various research used to write this book, and considering personal experience in working with those on death row, it seems that it would be more practical to simply place someone who has committed such a capital crime that would warrant the death penalty in prison for life rather than go to the extreme cost and effort involved in executing that person.

The hazards of maintaining death row facilities are extremely great. The reasons for this includes the housing of individuals who have been given a death sentence, as well as the extreme care that must be taken by correctional officers to maintain the security of such a unit.

Regardless of the moral issue that might be suggested in executing an inmate, the real issue that remains is a political one. The decision to use such a final judgment is up to the voter and the ballot box. As corrections professionals, the Federal Bureau of Prisons' statement that resonates is the following: "Until the laws of various states are changed, we must fulfill that law."

REFERENCES

American Correctional Association. 1989. *Managing Death-sentenced Inmates: A Survey of Practices.* Lanham, Maryland: American Correctional Association.

___. 1998. ACA Death Sentence Survey.

___. 1999. Death Row and the Death Penalty. *Corrections Compendium.* September. Vol. 24, No. 9.

___. 1999. Women in Correctional Leadership Course. Lanham, Maryland.

American Correctional Health Services Association. 1991. *Corhealth.* August/September/October.

Association of State Correctional Administrators. 1992. *Managing Capital Punishment Inmates.* Vol. VIII, No. 8.

Bureau of Justice Statistics. 1985. *Capital Punishment, 1984.* Washington, D.C.: Department of Justice.

___. 1987. *Capital Punishment, 1986.* Washington, D.C.: Department of Justice.

___. 1989. *Capital Punishment, 1988.* Washington, D.C.: Department of Justice.

___. 1996. *Capital Punishment, 1995.* Washington, D.C.: Department of Justice.

___. 1998. *Capital Punishment, 1997.* Washington, D.C.: Department of Justice.

California Department of Corrections. Regulations. General Institution Regulations, Public Information and Community Relations (nd).

CEGA Services. 1992. Confining the Condemned. *Corrections Compendium.* January.

Chicago Sun Times. 1996. Second Chance for 3 Inmates. June 15. Page 6, Metro Section.

Corrections Today. 1998. Correctional News Brief. Volume 60, No. 5 (August).

Criminal Justice Newsletter. 1998. Texas Law Makers Urge Executions. Vol. 29, No. 6. (March 17). Pace Publications.

Death Penalty Information Center. 1998. *Innocence and the Death Penalty.* Washington, D.C.: Death Penalty Information Center.

___. 1999. *Facts about the Death Penalty.* Washington, D.C.: Death Penalty Information Center.

Federal Bureau of Prisons. 1993. Death Penalty Policies. *Federal Register.* Vol. 58, No. 11 (January 19).

Florida Department of Corrections. 1999. Death Row Fact Sheet. August. www.dc.state.fl.us/oth/deathrow/index.html.

Frame, Randy. 1995. A Matter of Life and Death. *Christianity Today*. Vol. 39, No. 9 (August).

Haney, Craig and Mona Lynch. 1977. Regulating Prisons of the Future: A Psychological Analysis of a Supermax and Solitary Confinement. *New York University Review of Law and Social Change*. 23: 477.

Illinois Department of Corrections. 1997. Illinois Administrative Code. Effective July 1, 1996. Section 103.40 News Media.

Johnson, Robert. 1998. *Death Work: A Study of the Modern Execution Process*. 2d Edition. Belmont, California: Wadsworth.

Lancaster, Jennie. 1993. Management Issues for Female Inmates on Death Row. In *Female Offenders: Meeting Needs of a Neglected Population*. Lanham, Maryland: American Correctional Association.

Lauen, Roger J. 1997. *Positive Approaches to Corrections: Research, Policy, and Practice*. Lanham, Maryland: American Correctional Association.

Missouri Department of Corrections. 1996. Public Information Procedure. Jefferson City, Missouri: Missouri Department of Corrections.

___. 1997. *History of the Death Penalty in Missouri*. Jefferson City, Missouri: Missouri Department of Corrections.

Missouri House of Legislature. "Repeal of the Death Penalty." HB. 1096. Jefferson City, Missouri.

National Institute of Corrections' Prison Division and the National Institute of Corrections Academy. 1993. *Management of Death Row: A Special Issue Seminar*. Available from the NIC Information Center, Longmont, Colorado.

Office of Juvenile Justice and Delinquency Prevention. 1997. *Juvenile Offenders and Victims: 1997 Update on Violence*. Washington, D.C.: Office of Juvenile Justice and Delinquency Prevention.

Rhine, Edward, ed. 1998. *Best Practices: Excellence in Corrections*. Lanham, Maryland. American Correctional Association.

Riveland, Chase. 1999. *Supermax Prisons: Overview and General Considerations*. Washington, D.C.: National Institute of Corrections.

Salinas, Patti Ross and Tana McCoy. 1999. Management Issues Surrounding Women on Death Row. *Corrections Management*. 3(1). Winter.

Stewart, Richard. 1999. New Death Row to Have Books but No TV. *Houston Chronicle*. June 1999, page 36A.

Turpin, James and Donna Lyons. 1999. Criminal Justice Legislation. *Corrections Compendium*, Vol. 24, No. 2. February.

RELEVANT COURT CASES

Arave v. Creech, 507 U.S. 463 (1993)

Brisbon v. Lane, 857 F2d 1476 (7th Cir. 1988)

Coker v. Georgia, 97 S.Ct. 2861 (1977)

Daniels v. Zant, 494 F. Supp. 720 (M.D. Ga. 1980)

Fikes v. Alabama, 352 U.S. 191 (1957)

Ford v. Wainwright, 106 S.Ct. 2595 (1986)

Furman v. Georgia, 408 U.S. 238 (1972)

Gregg v. Georgia, 428 U.S. 153 (1976)

Groseclose v. Dutton, 788 F.2d 356 (6th Cir. 1986)

Harris v. Alabama, 513 U.S. 504 (1995)

Lockhart v. McCree, 476 U.S. 162 (1986)

Maynard v. Cartwright, 108 S.Ct. 1853 (1988)

McClesky v. Kemp, 107 S.Ct. 1756, 481 U.S. 279 (1987)

McCleskey v. Zant, 11 S.Ct. 1454 (1991)

McDonald v. Armontrout, 860 F.2d 1456 (1988)

Penry v. Lynaugh, 109 S.Ct. 2934 (1984)

Perry v. Louisiana, 106 S.Ct. 2595 (1990)

Powell v. Alabama, 287 U.S. 45 (1932)

Pulley v. Harris, 104 S.Ct. 3154 (1984)

Rust v. Gunter, 774 F.2d 1169 (8th Cir. 1985)

Sivak v. Murphy, 865 F.2d 265 (9th Cir. 1985)

Spaziano v. Flordia, 104 S.Ct. 3154 (1984)

Stanford v. Kentucky, 109 S.Ct. 2969 (1989)

Thompson v. Enomoto, 915 F.2d 1383 (9th Cir. 1990)

Thompson v. Oklahoma, 108 S.Ct. 2687, 487 U.S. 815 (1988)

Tison v. Arizona, 107 S.Ct. 1676 (1987)

Wainwright v. Witt, 469 U.S. 412 (1985)

Witherson v. Illinois, 391 U.S. 510 (1968)

Woodson v. North Carolina, 96 S.Ct. 2978 (1976)